EVERYTHING

GUIDE TO

COOKING FOR CHILDREN WITH DIABETES

Dear Reader,

I can remember my first visit to a supermarket in the days just after my daughter had been diagnosed with Type 1 (juvenile) diabetes. So intimidating were the aisles, I actually sobbed in the middle of the popcorn and snacks section. Food, you see, had—in my head—become the enemy. Carbs lingered around every corner. "Bad choices" stared me down at every pass. How carefree the job of feeding my family had been B.D. (before diabetes), I thought.

The good news was I learned that in today's world, food is no longer the enemy, and with good planning, some smart cooking, and the support of a good medical team, my daughter's life didn't have to be dramatically changed. In fact, I realized, diabetes might help bring my entire family to a better place. If I could learn to prepare fun, interesting, and healthy meals that *any* child or family would love and benefit from, wouldn't that be a good thing? This book is an effort to help you, the parent of a child with diabetes, do just that.

I hope that if you are new to diabetes, this book will help you with some ideas that will keep that supermarket trip from being so upsetting. If you've been dealing with a child with diabetes for some time, I hope it opens up some new ideas to you.

I hope you'll try and enjoy the recipes in this book. I hope some of them become family traditions. I hope you encourage your child to learn to cook them along with you. Because one day, diabetes will be cured, but we'll all still need to eat healthy. Happy Cooking!

Moira McCarthy

Welcome to the EVERYTHING Series!

These handy, accessible books give you all you need to tackle a difficult project, gain a new hobby, or even brush up on something you learned back in school but have since forgotten. You can choose to read from cover to cover or just pick out information from our four useful boxes.

 Alerts

Urgent warnings

 Facts

Important snippets of information

 **Essentials**

Quick handy tips

 **Questions**

Answers to common questions

When you're done reading, you can finally say you know **EVERYTHING®**!

PUBLISHER Karen Cooper

DIRECTOR OF ACQUISITIONS AND INNOVATION Paula Munier

MANAGING EDITOR, EVERYTHING® SERIES Lisa Laing

COPY CHIEF Casey Ebert

ACQUISITIONS EDITOR Brett Palana-Shanahan

DEVELOPMENT EDITOR Brett Palana-Shanahan

EDITORIAL ASSISTANT Hillary Thompson

EVERYTHING® SERIES COVER DESIGNER Erin Alexander

LAYOUT DESIGNERS Colleen Cunningham, Elisabeth Lariviere, Ashley Vierra, Denise Wallace

Visit the entire Everything® series at *www.everything.com*

THE

EVERYTHING®

Guide to Cooking for Children

WITH DIABETES

From everyday meals to holiday treats—
how to prepare foods your child will love to eat

Moira McCarthy with Leslie Young, MD

Avon, Massachusetts

An Everything® Series Book.
Everything® and everything.com® are regis-
tered trademarks of F+W Media, Inc.

Published by Adams Media, a division of F+W Media, Inc.
57 Littlefield Street, Avon, MA 02322 U.S.A.
www.adamsmedia.com

ISBN 10: 1-4405-0023-1
ISBN 13: 978-1-4405-0023-7

Printed in China.

J I H G F E D C B A

Library of Congress Cataloging-in-Publication Data
is available from the publisher.

This publication is designed to provide accurate and authoritative information with regard to the subject matter covered. It is sold with the understanding that the publisher is not engaged in rendering legal, accounting, or other
professional advice. If legal advice or other expert assistance is required, the
services of a competent professional person should be sought.
—From a *Declaration of Principles* jointly adopted by a Committee of the
American Bar Association and a Committee of Publishers and Associations

Many of the designations used by manufacturers and sellers to distinguish
their products are claimed as trademarks. Where those designations appear
in this book and Adams Media was aware of a trademark claim, the designations have been printed with initial capital letters.

This book is available at quantity discounts for bulk purchases.
For information, please call 1-800-289-0963.

To Lauren and to all the kids with Type 1.
May the cure come soon.

Acknowledgments

As always, I salute my daughter Lauren for the years and years of brave battle she's put up in the face of Type 1 diabetes; her sister and my daughter, Leigh, for being a good sport through it all; and my husband, Sean, for setting the healthy eating standard in our house. So, too, do I thank the many volunteers and staff of the Juvenile Diabetes Research Foundation International who give me hope and faith that one day, none of this will be necessary. In particular, I thank Heidi Daniels, Joana Casas, Bill Ahearn, Benita Shobe, Susan Sobers, Maryanne Jacobson, Cynthia Ford, Katie Clark, the Glass Family, the Bennett Family, Kristin Maresca, Jennifer Fishkind, Jessica Meltzer, Kassy "Marsha Brady" Helme, Andrea Hulke, Red and Marinda Maxwell, Renata Lanoix, and all those other great people who refuse to give up. Thanks also to Senator Edward Kennedy (D-MA) and his amazing staff for being a friend, supporter, and inspiration all these years to Lauren. You've made a wonderful difference in her life. And a special thanks to my friend Anne D'Angelo and family. You were so supportive all the years I've had to deal with this. It breaks my heart to welcome you to this world, but together, we can find the cure. Go to *www.jdrf.org* to learn more.

Contents

Introduction

Once you get past the diabetes diagnosis and the needles and the shots and the finger pricks, it's the main thing on your mind:

How and what am I going to feed this child?

Common knowledge tells you that when it comes to diabetes, it's all about the food. And in a way, it is. After all, from here on in, you'll need to count and study every single carbohydrate your child ingests and make a medical decision on how much insulin needs to be matched with that.

That's daunting. But the good news is this: Kids with diabetes can eat almost exactly the same as all children should eat (emphasize *should* there, good parent). That wasn't always the case. As little as a decade ago, there was no such thing as rapid-acting insulin, and children with diabetes were forced to eat on a meal plan and schedule, eating the exact same amount of carbs at the exact same time, day in and day out, with nary a change in that schedule.

But today, with pumps and rapid-acting insulin and continuous glucose monitors to manage it all, kids with diabetes are free to explore food choices almost the same as all other children. Heading to a birthday party? You can absolutely let him have a slice of that cake (as long as you know his blood glucose-to-carb ratio and then give the insulin for that). Planning a party yourself? You can go the traditional route, or better yet, be creative and make the food at that party more healthy but just as enjoyable, proving to all the guests that healthy can be fun and delicious.

As the following chapters show you, it's a good idea to work toward a healthy, balanced diet for your child with diabetes. True, there's no longer a need to deny him most foods. But if you can introduce foods that are special, interesting, and creative and yet still help your child have less of a blood glucose spike, a parent's got to say, "Why not?"

As you'll read, doctors now know that maintaining relatively stable blood sugars is key to a long, healthy life for anyone with diabetes. As a parent, you'll want to balance that with helping your child not feel denied. Teaching him that interesting meals and treats created at home can, in fact, be superior to some foods that are not as good for him will set the standard for his life, a standard that allows him to treat himself right while enjoying true treats. (Any parent who has ever brought sugar-free "jigglers" to a party will tell you: they are usually gobbled up while cupcakes are left behind. Who knew!)

Also because helping to prepare a meal can be pivotal in getting your child to eat it, this handy book calls out recipes your child can help prepare with you. Just look for the icon 🌀 next to the recipe name. And because nearly 40 percent of children with diabetes are also gluten-allergic, you'll find gluten-free recipes in this cookbook, highlighted with a gluten-free icon. **GF**

Roll up your sleeves, create some new foods, and see if you can't take your family on a new food adventure that's not just good for diabetes, but just plain good for you.

CHAPTER 1

Life, the Diabetes Diet, and the Pursuit of Normalcy

After, "He'll need shots for the rest of his life!" the biggest "OMG" moment for a parent of a child newly diagnosed with diabetes is, "How will I ever adapt to feeding my child a diabetes diet?" Indeed, from the day of diagnosis, food quickly becomes the center of your life. What to eat, what not to eat, what your aunt thinks he should eat, what your mother just knows he should never eat, and what the rest of the world is thinking as he is eating can take over your life, and your child's as well. The trick is to make it all seem somewhat normal. The good news is, for the most part and with some little tweaks, you can do just that.

What *Is* a "Diabetes Diet," Really?

There's a perception out there that the diabetes diet is bland, restrictive, and hard to manage. Thanks to a better understanding of how carbs and insulin interact, and thanks to better tools like pumps and rapid-acting insulin, this is no longer the case. Understanding this new freedom and yet making smart choices is the foundation of establishing a good diabetes diet.

It's Not as Different as You May Think

It might not be fair to call what most assume is the diabetes diet—a strict meal plan that can never be swayed from—a myth. Not too long ago, that was the way of life. As recently as the late 1990s, children who were diagnosed with diabetes were immediately placed on rigid and restricted diets. Parents were taught to think in terms of meal plans and planned snacks and to not sway from that at all.

 Fact

Rapid-acting insulin such as Humalog and NovoLog were approved for use in children circa 2000, giving parents the option of covering meals and snacks, thus allowing for more flexibility in eating plans.

With the advent of rapid-acting insulin, health providers and families alike began to realize that flexibility was possible. This meant that, for the first time, kids could truly have an ice cream when they wanted it, dig into a piece of cake at a party, and even—be still the heart of diabetes parents everywhere—skip a meal if they were so inclined. This was revolutionary. But the world has been slow to catch on. Most in the general population still assume kids must avoid all sugars and many carbs. You'll hear it, and you'll need to correct it. It's a new world of diabetes, kids, and food out there. But it's still vital to think healthy and smart.

 Alert

You need to prepare your child to respond when people say things like, "You're diabetic—you cannot eat that," because it will happen. Help them with a stockpile of polite answers like, "My plan allows this. Thank you for your concern."

Why You Need Not Advertise It

In the old days, parents would have to let everyone know that their child could only eat certain things, so they wouldn't be tempted to eat things that their insulin and plan could not cover. Hurray for the fact that those days are in the past! Which means, for the most part, that you don't need to advertise (at least not in a big way) any special dietary needs for your child.

True, you will still need to remind your child and your family and friends that she must match food with insulin, but for the most part, just about anything you would feed a child on a healthy diet without diabetes works for your child, too.

Technical Stuff

That's not to say this is all a snap. You, dear parent, will need to become an expert in nutrition, and do so quickly. Your child, too, will need to understand concepts that most children don't give a thought to. It's an old joke that the parent of a child with diabetes knows the carb count of every food on earth but has no idea where he is supposed to be at 3 P.M. Semitrue, but learning the technical stuff will lead to a more flexible life for your child.

The Meaning of Carbs

What is a carbohydrate? To put it in simple terms, carbs are the fuel that your body runs on. All energy in food comes from carbs, protein, and fatty acids. Carbs are the high-energy fuel that comes from sugars (simple carbs) and starches (complex carbs). All carbs interact with insulin in the body in the process of converting to fuel for the cells to use.

 Essential

A small yet complete book listing carbs of all foods is a must-have. Check the cooking section of your local bookstore and buy three copies—one for home, one for the glove compartment, and one for your child's diabetes bag.

Simple sugars are absorbed directly into the bloodstream fairly quickly after you eat them. Complex carbs digest first into sugar and then into glucose, taking a bit more time. Both types of carbs are the body's main source of energy. Everyone, including your child with diabetes, needs some carbs.

This is why, while some people will think, "Well, if I need insulin to match my carbs, couldn't I just avoid insulin by avoiding carbs?" this simply is not possible. Every body needs fuel to survive, particularly that of a growing child. Matching carbs to insulin as a way to mimic the actions of a normal-functioning pancreas is how a parent helps a child not just survive but thrive with diabetes on board.

The Meaning of the Glycemic Index

The glycemic index (GI) measures the speed at which your bloodstream absorbs the sugars in carbs against a mean of 100, which equals the speed of glucose (pure sugar) absorption. In other words, the GI ranks carbs based on their immediate effect on the pure sugar levels in the bloodstream.

 Question

Is there a place I can learn more about the glycemic index?
For more information about the GI and how to calculate the GI of specific foods, go to *www.diabetesnet.com*.

A carb that is ranked high on the GI is one that absorbs into the bloodstream quickly and causes a dramatic and immediate peak in glucose levels. In the diabetes world, this is called a spike. As you will learn later on in this book, while it's not a good idea to feed a child high-GI foods at all times, sometimes, with the right insulin planning, is perfectly acceptable.

A slow-release food is low on the GI and crests at much lower levels. Thus, energy levels remain constant for a long period of time and there are no spiked highs or precipitous lows from that food. A good mix of many low and moderate GI foods is a good choice for any diet, but we all can have a high GI or two from time to time.

How Insulin Does and Doesn't Work with Foods

Being the parent or caretaker of a child with diabetes means, quite literally, being their acting pancreas. You must learn not only what each type of insulin is and how it functions (fast acting, short acting; long duration, short duration), but also what each food means and how each reacts in your child's body. It's a lot to know, and it's no small feat to conquer this challenge. But with information, study, and practice, you can.

The Art of Carb Counting and Dosing

Notice the word "art" in place of what you may think of as "science." While figuring out the actual carb count of a food or meal is indeed scientific, knowing how your child's body reacts to each type of carb is truly art. Some foods cause huge spikes for some kids, but not for others. It takes time and practice to figure out the average expectation of a food's reaction in a body, weigh that against what you see happening in your child, and then assess and learn from each experience.

 Essential

All hail the mighty log book! Keeping a detailed log book that tracks which foods your child eats and how his body responds to them is a vital step toward mastering the task of matching insulin and food for your child. Get one and do it, starting now.

Carb counting and dosing takes time—and expert advice—to figure out. You should be working with your diabetes team to do this. Even if you've been dealing with diabetes for years, remember: A body changes, and so does its response to foods and insulins. Break out the log book again if you've been at it for a while and watch closely, again, for how your child's body responds in its own unique way to different foods. Let's say you notice, three times in a row, that when your daughter eats pasta, she spikes three hours later. After observing this pattern you will be able to make an insulin decision to match that information (such as a square wave bolus on a pump or an added shot a couple of hours later for those on shots). In other words, you learn and react based on experience.

What about Sugar?

You've heard it so many times you can almost laugh: "Can't you just stay away from refined sugars?" This myth most likely comes from how people with Type 2 diabetes tend to battle their disease.

 Alert

Type 1 and Type 2 diabetes are so completely different they don't even share the same genetic makeup. Type 1 is an autoimmune disease; Type 2 is metabolic. Be clear about that to others, who may not understand.

The fact is, while sugar does spike the blood sugar, kids with diabetes can have it just like other kids can (that means, within reason and in a healthy amount). The common perception that (1) your child needs to stay away from jelly doughnuts and (2) if he just does that he'll be fine, is simply not true. Because again, with understanding and planning, a jelly doughnut or any other treat is not out of the realm of possibility. Letting your child know this and allowing him treats may help keep him from feeling different, left out, or wanting to sneak something you could have let him have anyway.

Spikes and How to Deal with Them

There will be no avoiding the fact that some foods—most foods, in fact—will make your child's blood sugar spike in one way or another. It's the knowing, though, that will help you manage this while still serving some great meals and treats. When rapid-acting insulin came on the market, parents cheered because finally, instead of having to give kids a shot at least a half hour and sometimes hours before a meal and then demanding the child eat exactly the carbs they'd been given the shot for, parents could now wait to see what the child wanted to eat and give a shot just for that. In some cases, parents would even wait until a meal was done, count the carbs the child had ingested, and then bolus (or give a shot) for that. But soon, doctors and parents realized something was happening: While this method gave more freedom, a child who was eating without any rapid (meal-covering) insulin onboard would spike to a point that would not be corrected by the usual dose.

 Fact

While most kids have the same carb-to-insulin ratio all day long, some children have different ones at different times of day. Talk to your medical team if you see spikes at certain times of the day.

Some parents split the difference and give half a meal bolus before the meal (usually about ten minutes before helps the insulin get ahead of the food) and the remainder needed at the end of the meal. Of course, you need to talk to your medical team before trying anything like this.

You may discover, too, that there are some red-light foods for your child that make her blood sugar go high no matter how carefully you measure out the food and the insulin. For some children, it's syrup. For others, it's slushes. If you find a food that makes your child spike high no matter what you do, you may want to consider limiting it to a very rare usage. Try to find replacements your child likes, and explain to her why you are looking to limit that food. Point out, too, that she can still have many other foods, just not that one.

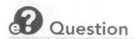 **Question**

Can a high-spiking food ever be served to my child?
Yes. Just plan on checking blood sugars again about two hours after the meal and making adjustments in insulin doses as needed at that time. But don't do it all of the time.

Why is it important to avoid spikes? Because science now shows that even a child in good control can suffer long-term complications from too many spikes. Once in a while is fine, but certainly not on a daily basis.

Saying Yes and Saying No

In the beginning of life with diabetes you may think "no" will be your most-used word. But in fact, you can say yes to many things, and even open up your child's mind to saying yes to some meals and treats he may not have considered in his prediabetes life.

For Beginners, Start Without Scaring

You simply cannot take a child from Oscar Mayer wieners to tofu on a field of wild greens in a day and not expect her (and the rest of the family) to balk. Whether you are a newly diagnosed family or a long-time diabetes family looking to tune up, baby steps should be your motto.

Start first by considering this: Does your child have to eat a school lunch? If yes, meet with the school to figure out the carb counts of meals and which ones you might want to avoid (you can compromise and let her eat the school lunch most of the time). If your child is willing to consider bagging it, promise interesting and fun meals, and point out the added bonuses: no waiting in a lunch line means more socializing time, and homemade meals means more selection.

 Essential

Don't be an alarmist and demand your child and family change everything. Go slow, think things over, and consider everyone's feelings.

Next, look at some easy fixes at home. Try replacing higher-carb condiments like salad dressing with low- or no-carb substitutes and see if your kids even notice. Give it a month, then point out the change you made. This may open your up child and family to more changes with less fear.

For Long-Timers, Encouraging New Habits

For kids who have been on pumps for a while, some habits may have developed. With the glee of getting off the old-fashioned meal plan came much freedom. And in the end, while you want freedom, you want healthy choices, too—*just like any other child.* No, you don't have to put your child back on a meal plan. Rather, look to serve him some new and interesting (and low-carb and low-GI) meals and don't tell him for a while. Again, once he likes it, you can spill the beans and suggest more ideas. But remember, do leave in the special treats and loves (more of how to make this work in Chapter 2). In the end, like anything else, adapting to better eating is all about balancing—health, happiness, and a feeling of being a normal kid.

Public Perception

Everyone, you realize, has an opinion on the diabetes diet. They talk about their Aunt Sue who now only eats whole-grain cereal and "hardly needs insulin at all." They point to their friend's father who ate too much "sugared food" and lost a foot. You know this is all hearsay and you know you understand what is best for your child. Dealing with this is a start to shifting to healthy living in a practical way.

What Folks Will Say

"But she can have all the fruit she wants without insulin because it's 'natural sugar,' right?" For just about ever now, you and your child will be charged with explaining what she is eating, why she is eating it, and why you are or are not worried. True, such comments are an invasion of your privacy and there are times when if you could just shoot laser beams out of your eyes it would all be better, but think of it this way: A little education goes a long way.

So every time someone says something like, "I wanted to let you know because I think you should—I saw your child with diabetes *eating a candy bar!*" think of it this way: That family is lucky to not know all the information you know (since they've been spared a diagnosis of diabetes) and is lucky to have you to set them straight so they won't say the same thing to another family.

What You Should Say

The best response, while you'd really like to just scream sometimes, is to calmly explain that with Type 1 diabetes and new insulin and tools like pumps, you are happy that you can now feed your child in a healthy way and with few restrictions.

And what of the people who will tell you of folks they know who have "gotten off insulin" but are eating certain foods? Your answer to that can be short and to the point. "My child has Type 1, which is an autoimmune disease and no matter what he eats, his body will not make insulin. I appreciate your input, but please understand it is not an option for my child or any other child with Type 1 diabetes."

CHAPTER 2

Getting Started

Whether you are the parent of a newly diagnosed child or of a child who has been living with diabetes for a while, working toward a healthy (but still fun) family menu isn't something that you can accomplish in a day. Getting started means looking carefully at what you have in your cabinets now, how your family eats currently, and what you can do to keep everyone happy yet healthy. It's all about study, planning, and quiet implementation.

A Quiet Shift (or Stealth Meal Planning)

Resist the urge to shout from the rooftops, "We are changing our eating habits and changing them *now*!" Kids like to think life just goes along as it should, and adults don't like to feel that they are being forced to change their ways. Instead, quietly find ways to make changes, and make them a few at a time. You may just find that your family barely notices.

Filling the Cabinets Without Balks

Your first step toward better cooking and eating is doing a complete inventory of your cabinets and fridge. What are the staples? Is almost everything premade or packaged? If your answer is yes, consider moving back to the source point of foods, and consider making some smart but acceptable-to-all replacements.

Fill containers in your cabinets with things like whole almonds, Kashi cereal (great for snacking!), brown rice, and wheat pasta. In the fridge, keep a large container of fresh chopped fruit and some low-fat vanilla yogurt for easy access. Fresh veggies like baby carrots and cut bell peppers are a must as well.

 Essential

Invest today in Tupperware-like containers for most foods. Removing the original boxes and storing foods in an attractive way will sway your family toward feeling good about your changes. It's easier and good for the earth, since you can buy in bulk and cut down on packaging.

But don't throw away all the good stuff. Make batches of low-carb cookies (see Chapter 13 for ideas) and always have "free foods" on hand (see Chapter 15). Keep some guilty pleasures for each family member on hand as well. After all, life is about going nuts sometimes.

Enlisting the Family Without Fanfare

Of course, you won't want to do this without your family knowing at all. Finding a way to get them onboard and being sure to keep their feelings (and likes and dislikes) in mind is tricky but worth the effort. So start like this: Ask each family member to make a list of the meals and foods they love the most, from dinners to snacks to lunch choices. Ask them to also list a few foods they might be hesitant about but would be willing to try at least once. Then, ask them to choose two or three must-have treats that they cannot do without. This list will be your starting point.

Once you have those lists, study this cookbook (and others) and find recipes that match up with what your family tells you they love.

Got a fried-chicken aficionado? There are plenty of healthy recipes for a meal that's just like fried chicken out there (see Chapter 14 for a start). Want to make sure your sweet-tooth child has something to fill that craving? Find some free foods that match up to what he loves. And then, stretch the whole thing out. Find some interesting foods and recipes that may just surprise your family. And shhh! Don't tell them it's healthy. Rather, present it as a special over-the-top meal. What they don't know cannot freak them out.

 Alert

> Remember, going too far will only backfire. If your child tells you he simply must have Twinkies, work on adding one or two a week into his plans. Total denial never works. It's all about moderation.

As you make these changes, take note of what they are attracted to for snacks, and which meals they like the most. From there, you'll be able to make decisions about other snacks and meals that match their taste buds. Sure, it takes time and energy, but in the end, it will be worth it.

Small, Easy, and Quick Fixes

Little things mean a lot. It's an old adage, and certainly one that holds true when it comes to making your family's eating habits healthier. There are little things you can do from the start that will immediately impact your family's healthy habits.

First, forget the butter when it comes to many types of cooking. A can of Pam goes a long way. If you are greasing a pan of any kind with anything else, end that practice today (unless a recipe demands it). Your family will never even notice, and you will easily cut out grams of fat. Second, if you have not already, move to 1% milk. Milk is made so well today that the 1% really does taste great. Chances are, your family will not even notice and if they do, in time, they'll come to feel that anything more than 1% tastes too thick.

For snacking, while you want to move to whole foods whenever you can, at least move to baked chips instead of the traditional chips. The carb count doesn't vary that much, but what's in them as a whole does, and that makes a difference. Remember, you need to be heart-health conscious with a child with diabetes (and with anyone, really). Baked chips are yummy, too. Most people find they prefer them once they've tried them.

 Fact

If you have a toddler in the house, you'll need some whole milk. Toddlers need the fat and bulk provided by whole milk (unless there is a family history of obesity, hyperlipidemia, or heart disease). Talk to your pediatrician before making any changes in diet if you have small children in the house.

You can also make changes as simple as making sure you're stocking the house with white tuna packed in water rather than white tuna in oil or chunk light tuna. White tuna in oil, even when completely drained, packs a full five additional grams of fat into each serving. And chunk light, even though it has that word "light" in there, tends to have more fat than solid tuna. Solid white also has three times the omega-3 fats (read: good fats) that chunk light has.

And here's another simple shift that can make eating healthy seem more fun and even good for your mind and soul: Go back to eating as a family. Too many families today, because of sports schedules, hectic work days, and life in general, have moved away from sitting down at a traditional table for a traditional family meal. Make a rule that at least four times a week you will eat together as a family. Enjoy discussions, catch up on each other's lives, and talk about the world. This will make eating a meal about much more than the food, and might just add to your health and happiness. Oh yes, and try to eat breakfast as a family at least twice a month (imagine that!) Sometimes, simple changes around meals can make eating right a pleasure.

 Question

Should I do all this completely on my own?
One of the "benefits" of having a child with diabetes in the house is that you have access to a nutritionist who understands your needs. If you have not met with her in a while, make an appointment and go over your new plan.

Becoming a Planner

No one really wants to obsess over meal planning. There is something about feeling spontaneous with food and meals that makes it taste all the better. But with good planning as a foundation, that spontaneity can come without the cost of poor nutrition choices.

The Art (and Benefit) of Planning Your Week

Let's face it, in today's world, most families fly by the seat of their pants when it comes to meals. Many who are in charge of the family shopping stop by a convenience store every day or so and plan as the days go by. So how about taking a step back, considering weekly planning, and seeing what it will do not only for providing a good, balanced week of food for your family, but less stress for the shopper and meal planner? Admittedly, it takes time in the beginning, but in time you should have a plan that works for you and your family and makes things easy.

The art of planning a week of meals comes in learning to make decisions ahead of time. As you work toward being a good planner, build up a recipe file of your family's favorite meals and snacks. Then, one evening a week, sit down and plan out your meals, being careful to vary them so your family does not get bored. From this list will come your shopping list for the week. Check your cabinets for what needs restocking and then do one large shopping trip, which will cut down your convenience store visits and save you cash in the long run. Be sure to consider your schedule and your family's schedule when making a decision for each day's meals. Will you be rushed on a particular evening? A meal that you can prepare ahead or quickly pull together is your best bet. Will it be a week of fast breakfasts? You'll want to make sure you have plenty handy.

 Alert

Purchasing in bulk is a great idea for long-lasting staples. You'll save time and money. But for perishable items like celery, you'll end up tossing more away. Be selective about bulk purchases.

Balancing a Week (and Making Room for Extras)

When planning out the week, you'll want to be sure to balance out what your family will be eating. Don't go with red meat every night; rather, vary the main course from meat to chicken to fish to even vegetarian. Such variety will be sure to excite your family and, rather than have them thinking, "They are making me eat all this health stuff" will make them think, "Wow, the food around here is getting positively exotic." Just be sure to balance it in a way that is doable for the cook(s).

The same goes for school lunches. While it's true that some children love to pack the same lunch day after day (and this is great for a kid with diabetes since you'll know the carb count and exactly how it affects your child's blood sugars), other kids want variety. In that case, you'll want to plan out the week ahead of time so you have what you need on hand. As for breakfasts, you'll want to plan for and have on hand fast and healthy breakfast choices for harried mornings as well as ingredients for a more sophisticated breakfast on days when you can make that work.

 Essential

Doubling up a freezable recipe can be a lifesaver for the family cook(s). Usually it is just as easy to make twice as much of something. Freeze half, and you'll have a future night off from cooking without sacrificing a good choice.

And what about the goodies? Plan ahead and bake or cook some special desserts that are healthy yet seem decadent. And let's say there's a special day coming up (report cards or birthdays, for instance). Let the person of honor choose a special menu, from soup to nuts to dessert, a week beforehand. That way you can plan, be ready, and even add some crazy foods for that special day. While you *can* match insulin with food at any time, if you are going to have, say, a dinner that's over the top, you may want to choose a lower-carb and healthier lunch and breakfast that day. Or, if you know you'll all want pancakes on a special day, plan on a lighter dinner for that evening. It's all about balance, just as it is for anyone.

Tools You Must Have

We've already talked about the need for plastic containers to store food in bulk and a book of basic carb counts for all foods, but there are more tools to make life easier when planning to cook well for a family and a child with diabetes. Measuring spoons and cups are a must, and a good food scale is a bonus. You won't need them all forever, but until you get a good feel for what six ounces of beef or a half cup of rice looks like on a plate, you'll want to measure it out so your insulin dose is precise to the amount of food you are serving. And really, in time, you'll come to be able to eye amounts (although your nutritionist will tell you that measuring can never be wrong.)

Another must is good products for carrying lunch to school. If you want your child to enjoy healthy foods, you need to be sure that the food you pack will stay crisp and fresh. It may be an investment at first, but a good insulated lunch bag and containers that are sturdy but easy to open and close will make your child's meal all the more palatable.

One big item that can really help with your planning is extra freezer space. If you have an older freezer or can afford a small extra one, set it up in your basement or garage to store prepared meals and other items. Having them on hand will make it easier to serve great meals, even on a night when you are late from work, had to stop for an eye exam, and still need to make it to your child's play rehearsal. Preparation and freezing makes you look good.

 Fact

Most caregivers of kids with diabetes do not measure foods very often. If you are finding that your child is experiencing some unexplained highs, go back to measuring for a week and see if you have simply lost sight of what a serving really is.

Understanding Food Labels

Parents of children with diabetes often report a completely overwhelmed feeling the first time they visit a food market after their child's diagnosis. This is because the sea of food labels before you—something you most likely long ignored—now begs for your attention. Learning to read labels can help make meals healthier.

Labels 101

Thankfully, the Food and Drug Administration (FDA) has standardized food labels so you can know what to expect. But that doesn't mean they are easy to read. First, always look closely at two things: the serving size *and* the servings per container. Sometimes it's easy to assume that a package contains just one serving, when in fact it does not. When you see that, for instance, a can of soup provides two and a half servings, you realize that simply looking at the carb count or fat grams listed on the label is not enough. You'll need to figure out how much of it you will use per person, and then do the math.

 Essential

Don't be embarrassed to carry a small calculator with you to the store for a while, or even forever. The breakdowns can be convoluted, and sometimes, technical help just makes things easier.

Next, you'll want to carefully read the carb count and make sure you know what it is per serving. When it comes to matching insulin with carbs, don't sweat the breakdown of sugars and carbs. For your needs, a carb is a carb is a carb and each type needs insulin. As for fiber, it is good to put more fiber in your child's meal plan (and yours as well). Fiber makes everything more healthy. However, even if you've heard friends talk about diets in which fiber wipes out carbs, do not make this assumption with your child. Talk to your nutritionist, but still plan on insulin for every carb.

Labels for Foods That Go into Recipes

Here is where your measuring cups and spoons as well as your calculator will come in handy. Add to them a notebook you keep with your cookbooks and you'll be ready to roll. The first time you make a recipe for which you do not have the nutritional breakdown (say, a great creation of your own), you'll need to count up and keep track of every carb you put into the recipe. At the end, divide the finished product into servings, and then divide the total carb count by the number of servings to find the carbs-per-serving amount. By keeping this information on file, you'll only need to do that extra work once, and next time, you can whip up that home-created favorite with confidence, knowing you're feeding your child well and accounting for everything you put into the recipe.

In the end, you'll find that while planning takes time at the start, it makes life easier down the road. Now that's a healthy plan.

CHAPTER 3

To Meal Plan or Not

Not so long ago—less than a decade—a child diagnosed with diabetes was immediately put onto a rigid and definitive meal plan.
Each meal and snack was planned out down to the last carb and exact
mealtimes, and a child (and his parents) had to stick to that. Recently,
with pumps and rapid-acting insulin, that has changed. But experts still
believe that the child on a well-planned eating program is the one who
does best. How do you balance what is best for her body with what makes
her feel best about life?

The Old Way

The old way was based, for the most part, on having to help the body
react to the different peaks of insulin varieties that children were given.
The standard meal plan was precise and hard to stick to, and yet, that
was what was done.

Traditional Meal Plan and Why It Was Done

Traditional meal plans were broken down in pretty much the same
way across the board: three meals and three snacks with each meal fea-
turing a serving of each food group, and each snack containing about
15g of carb (a double snack if extra activity was expected). Children had
to be fed at exactly the same times every day, and rarely, if ever, at other

times. Needless to say, it was hard to get a child of any age to adapt to such a life.

If, for example, Thanksgiving dinner was coming up and the family was expecting to eat at 2 P.M., parents would have to begin planning days in advance to make that work. Something as simple as a school lunchtime being changed would send shivers of fear down the spine of a parent.

 Fact

> Many parents of newly diagnosed children, presented with the classic meal plan, recognized it as similar to the classic Weight Watchers meal plan of the time. It was well rounded and healthy, but rigid.

And yet, even to this day, parts of the meal plan make sense. With everything around diabetes being so hard to put your finger on (since the weather, stress, changes in activity, even a test that day can affect a child's blood sugar), the discipline of serving planned and expected meals and being aware of carb totals and ingredients take some of the guesswork out of figuring out the daily treatment of a child with diabetes.

Rapid-Acting Insulin and the Advent of a New Plan

Or, should we say the plan-less revolution? For families who had been dealing with the regimented meal plan for years, the introduction of rapid-acting insulin, be it by needle, pen, or pump, meant a whole new way of living. As many medical teams told families to watch what their child eats but to let him eat like any other child, the glee of being free from the anchor of a meal plan led many families to go, as some would say, hog wild. After all, if you've forced a child to eat at exact times every day for years (and exact amounts, no more and no less) and suddenly you can just go with the flow, you're going to go with a heck of a lot of flow.

So the motto came to be embraced and embraced quickly: A carb is a carb is a carb. Families rejoiced as they let kids eat breakfast late (after having to drag them out of bed and feed them at exactly 7:30 every morning for years). So, too, did they smile when they heard the once-horrifying bells of an ice cream truck, because no longer did they have to hope that truck would only show up at exactly 8 P.M. or at the exact moment a child experienced a low. Those first years of rapid-acting insulin were giddy times. But like anything, a balance had to come.

 **Question**

Did nutritionists promote complete freedom from meal plans at this time?
Some did, but most did so with caveats: While families finally had the ability to cover treats and skip meals, many experts warned that some planning and balance would be best.

Finding a Balance Between the Two

While it is true that rapid-acting insulin leads to more freedom and choices and less stress, most diabetes experts now agree that it's best to have some kind of plan, even if it is just there to ignore from time to time. Most nutritionists agree that the ideal way to treat blood sugars in a child with diabetes is with the combination of a set meal plan and rapid-acting insulin. That said, almost no parents today are doing exactly that. After all, although the rigidity of the set meal plan may lead to a better assessment of where blood sugars are going, it also can lead to eating disorders at the worst and an obsession with food (and the control of it) at the least. It's not easy being a child on such a meal plan, and since raising a child with diabetes is about treating the whole child—physically, psychologically, and socially—parents, with the help of their medical team, need to look at the entire picture and come to a compromise.

So how to find a balance? The best bet is to think the way you would for any healthy child. For the most part, children need regular meals and regular snacks. Set a goal of three healthy meals a day and allow for snacks as the mood hits, but not too many every day. Think variety, health, and not too, too many carbs. By setting that as your base and allowing yourself to hop off it from time to time (just as any parent of any child would), you'll set a standard that your child should be able to not only live with, but learn by. Still, while it's true that you expect to serve three square meals a day, what if you are invited to a brunch? There is no reason you cannot skip breakfast with your child, head to brunch, and even let him overindulge a bit, making sure you count the carbs and cover them with insulin. Would you do that every day? No, but neither would you do so for any child. Point out to your child that you are treating him almost the same as you would a child without diabetes.

 Essential

If you've had your child on a strict meal plan and he is acting out by doing things like sneaking foods, it's time to make a change. Any food can be fit into a child's diabetes plan. There is no need to totally deny.

Members of the Meal-Plan Team

You, dear parent, should not be alone in this mission. In fact, planning out meals—from what will be served and when to how and why—is a big team effort, with a special part for each person. Make sure you have your team onboard every step of the way.

Why Every Child Needs a Nutritionist

Long ago, it was a given that every child with diabetes visited a nutritionist as many as four times a year. In recent years, thanks to cutbacks in health insurance coverage, some newly diagnosed children only see a nutritionist once a year—or in some cases, only once after being diagnosed. This is not a good pattern, as all children with diabetes (and their parents) need a nutritionist who specializes in Type 1 diabetes guiding them. Why? Because it's complicated, takes years to learn, and can be stressful. A good nutritionist will help you navigate these waters from the start.

 Question

What if there is no nutritionist with Type 1 diabetes experience in my area?
If this is the case, see if you can find a nutritionist who will consult via phone with another who does. Nutritionists who only deal with Type 2 are not fully trained to help with your child.

Your nutritionist can help you consider which foods and in what amounts work best for your growing child with diabetes. She should not be seen as the diabetes food police. Rather, she should be an expert voice who helps you and your child fit into life those things you want to fit, offering you ideas, insulin bolus suggestions, and always working as a part of your endocrine team to keep your child well and healthy.

The Parent's Role

Mom and Dad (or either/or if only one is around) have a special role on the meal-planning team: you are the protector and provider. It will be your job to not only make sure the foods your child wants and needs are within reach, but to prepare them in ways that will be palatable to her. At the same time, if you see something in your child's meal plan that just isn't working right, you are the one who needs to go to bat for your child. Some nutritionists will assign a child a set amount of carbs to be consumed per meal. This is simply not necessary, and really should only be treated as a guideline.

Most parents know you don't want a child with diabetes to consume 200g of carb at each meal. It's just too much (although that's not to say it would be too much at some special event). Let your instincts guide you. Feed your child a meal you see as reasonable for any child, count up the carb totals, and let that be a measure. But again, let your child's needs lead the way. She can voice her desires; you can give her what she needs while still working with the team. Eventually, most parents of kids with diabetes come to be experts. That does not mean, however, that your child should never see a nutritionist again. If you are years into this, consider checking back in at turning points such as starting high school sports, going to college, or during challenging hormonal times. The nutritionist can help you figure things out.

 Alert

If your child complains about being hungry all the time, he clearly needs more carbs. Let your team know that you want to make this change and ask for input. But in the end, go with your instincts and give your child what he needs.

The Child's Role

Often when a child is first diagnosed with diabetes a parent wonders, "Do I really need to drag him along to yet another appointment" (this time with a nutritionist)? The answer is absolutely yes. Why? Because the real leader of the nutrition and meal-planning team should be your child. True, he's too young to make decisions on his own, and that's why you are there to support him. But he needs to see, from day one, that his voice and desires matter in this process. Keep in mind that until a cure is found, your child needs to learn how to be an advocate for his own needs, and this is an important first step toward that.

Before each meeting with the nutritionist (and even from time to time before you do weekly shopping), encourage your child to think about what he's been eating, what he is tired of, and what he'd like to see added to his daily plans. Then take action. Show your child how you can make it work—within reason. Of course, there may be times you have to say no. Some children spike out of control with some things, and they just have to go. Sweetened soda is an example. There is no solid reason for needing it, and most children (if not all) should not have it. Help your child understand that you would not want him drinking soda even if he did not have diabetes, and that while you are making the decision based on spikes in blood sugars, you really would make it anyway. In fact, this is one case where the entire family can be expected to toe the line as well. Solidarity goes a long way with a child with diabetes.

 Fact

Children with diabetes who learn to voice their concerns and see that they are listened to have more of a chance of growing into adults who know how to get the help they need in life with diabetes.

The Role of the Rest of the Family

Siblings and even extended family members can all be a part of the team—albeit a distant part. It is important to let siblings know that you will not force them to completely change their lives because of diabetes in the house. However, the opportunity to help them eat more healthy meals and choose better snacks is an opportunity for a life lesson for them, too. Should a sister be gobbling down candy endlessly even if her brother has Type 1? No. But neither should she be if her brother does not have Type 1. If you had developed some bad family eating habits before diabetes came along, take this as a chance to help everyone. It's not a punishment; it's an opportunity.

In and around holidays, grandparents and aunts and uncles as well as cousins can help by not making food the center of every event. Come up with fun games, crafts, and other things to fill the holidays rather than just giant dessert buffets and foodfests. You may be surprised how much everyone enjoys being part of this team.

 **Essential**

Family members who can buy into things like having birthday party loot bags filled with small toys instead of candy are helping in a special and simple way. Encourage them to do so whenever possible.

Keeping Tabs

As much as you don't want your nutritionist to be the diabetes police, neither do you want to come across to your child that way. However, a good assessment of what she is eating and how it is affecting her is a necessary part of life with diabetes.

Food Journals: Use Them but Don't Abuse Them

Making insulin work with food is all about patterns. In fact, the only way you can truly know how certain carbs react with insulin in your child's body is to watch what happens, not once, not even twice, but three times. Of course, there is no way you can record all this in your memory, so you will need to keep a food journal.

 **Question**

Do I need an official food journal?
No, a simple notebook that you keep on hand will do. However, there are a wealth of food journals available at no cost online that would allow you to keep it all in your computer One simple one can be found at *www.lunch withlennie.co.uk*.

Begin tracking snacks and meals (including meals in this cookbook). Write down the blood sugar before the meal, what the insulin dose was (and the carb ratio) and then what the postprandial blood sugar is (this is a blood sugar check done two hours after a meal is complete). Look for trends that will tell you if you are over or underbolusing for that food, and if your child tends to spike from it. The information you will glean does not mean you'll have to remove the food from a plan; it simply shows you what special steps you'll have to take for your child when he enjoys that food.

So when can a parent go too far? Once you are well into your diabetes life, there will be no need to write down everything a child eats. In fact, in time, a food journal will only need to be reviewed and updated a couple of times a year at most. Don't get bogged down in watching and planning. Be conscientious, but not overreactive.

Recording Your Child's Reaction to Foods

So you get the information suggested above. How do you keep it and what do you do with it? Let's say you've discovered a great new healthy pizza recipe. Pizza has always been a food that messes with your daughter's blood sugars, and you are hoping this will help. Prepare the meal and record her reactions as suggested in the previous section. Be sure to take into account any special circumstances each day. For example, if she played hockey for an hour before the meal, her reaction could partially be due to the activity, and that needs to be considered. Once you've served the meal a few times with few variables, look for patterns. If she seems to be ending up a few hours later within her target blood sugar range, you've hit on the perfect insulin dose for this meal. But don't pat yourself on the back for too long. Doses tend to change annually or even more often during growth spurts. Check again if you see something questionable happen. These recordings will help you help your child enjoy all foods and, more important, understand what all foods mean to her.

Any Such Thing as Too Free?

As stated earlier in this chapter, families can go too far over to the do what you want side of eating. Again, it's a good idea to put aside your feelings about diabetes and think instead of how you would want to feed any child.

Coming Back Around Without Stress

So you got your child on the pump and had a two-year food free-for-all and now you know it's time to pull in the reins. Do it slowly and quietly. Cook new meals without comment and offer up healthy snacks, slowly removing the "bad" ones. See if your child likes it, and work to make him happy and balanced.

Sometimes a Kid Just Needs to Be a Kid

It's Halloween. Or New Year's Eve, and you are at a family party with a giant buffet. Or your daughter just won a dance competition and the prize is a giant frosted cookie. What is a diabetes parent to do? Sometimes, a kid just needs to be a kid. Since you know your child's body and insulin needs, just let it go sometimes. Let her overdo it for one day or one night. We all do, and we all survive. Just remind her: healthy families don't do that all the time. And in the end, find awesome recipes that feel special to her and seem decadent. That's the goal of the following chapters. Hopefully, your kid can just be a kid and love these. Until the cure, parents have no other choice.

CHAPTER 4

Super Day Starters
(Breakfasts That Set the Stage
for the Entire Day)

Egg Clouds on Toast

*For cinnamon French-style toast, sprinkle ¼ teaspoon cinnamon and
½ teaspoon powdered sugar (less than 10 calories; less than 2 calories
if using Whey Low Powder) over the top of the clouds.*

INGREDIENTS

2 egg whites

½ teaspoon sugar

1 cup water

1 tablespoon frozen apple juice
   concentrate

1 slice reduced-calorie oat bran
   bread, lightly toasted

1. In a metal bowl, beat the egg whites
   until they thicken. Add the sugar
   and continue to beat until stiff peaks
   form.

2. In a small saucepan, heat the water
   and apple juice concentrate over
   medium heat until it just begins to
   boil; reduce heat and allow mixture
   to simmer. Drop the egg whites by
   the teaspoonful into the simmering
   water. Simmer for 3 minutes, then
   turn the egg white "clouds" over
   and simmer for an additional 3
   minutes.

3. Ladle the clouds over the bread and
   serve immediately.

SERVES 1

Calories: 120 | Carbohydrates: 19g | Fat: 1g |
Sodium: 200mg | Fiber: 3g

Homemade Breakfast Sausage Patties

*You can omit the maple syrup and add
your own blend of herbs and spices.*

INGREDIENTS

1 pound lean ground pork

¼ cup bread crumbs

2 tablespoons cream

2 teaspoons pure maple syrup

2 teaspoons grated orange zest

2 teaspoons finely chopped fresh
parsley

⅛ teaspoon dried sage

½ teaspoon red pepper flakes

½ teaspoon salt

½ teaspoon freshly ground black
pepper

1½ tablespoons canola oil

1. In a medium-sized bowl, use your hands to mix together all of the ingredients until completely blended. Divide into 12 equal portions.

2. Place a nonstick sauté pan over medium heat. Wearing plastic gloves, gently form each patty about ½ inch thick and 2 inches in diameter. Working in batches, cook the patties on each side for about 5 minutes, or until they are golden brown. (Make sure they are cooked all the way through). Serve immediately.

SERVES 6

Calories: 260 | Carbohydrates: 5g | Fat: 20g |
Sodium: 270mg | Fiber: 0g

Scroddled Eggs

*Scroddled eggs are just barely mixed,
so the white and yellow portions are still visible in the finished product.*

INGREDIENTS

8 eggs

1 tablespoon olive or vegetable oil

½ teaspoon salt

⅛ teaspoon pepper

Eggs with History

Back in the Great Depression, customers at diners would ask for "scroddled" eggs because they couldn't be made with powdered egg. The white and yellow color of the partially beaten eggs can only be produced by using fresh eggs, which is not the case for traditional scrambled eggs or omelets.

1. Place eggs in medium bowl. Beat with a fork just until yolks are broken and mixture is slightly frothy. Do not overbeat; the yolks and whites should not be combined.

2. Heat medium nonstick skillet over medium heat. Add oil and swirl it around pan. Pour in eggs and sprinkle with salt and pepper. Cook, shaking pan occasionally and running a heatproof spatula around the edges of the eggs, until set.

3. Carefully turn eggs with a large spatula and cook until second side is set. Eggs should be visibly white and yellow. Cut into quarters to serve.

SERVES 4

Calories: 180 | Carbohydrates: 1g | Fat: 13g |
Sodium: 430mg | Fiber: 0g

Mixed-Berry–Filled Omelet

You can vary the berries you choose by season and availability in the market. After the berries have macerated in the sugar, they will give up some juice, which you can use as a sauce on your omelet.

INGREDIENTS

¼ cup fresh blueberries

¼ cup fresh raspberries

1 tablespoon Splenda

1 teaspoon grated orange zest

1 teaspoon buttery spread or margarine

4 eggs

¼ cup 1% milk

Salt and freshly ground black pepper to taste

What Is Macerating?

Macerating is the act of softening an object by soaking it in liquid. The principle is similar to marinating meats.

1. Mix the berries, Splenda, and orange zest. Let macerate for 30 minutes. Heat the buttery spread or margarine in a nonstick pan over medium flame.

2. Whisk the eggs and milk together. Pour into the hot pan and cook until the mixture just begins to set.

3. Spoon the berries in a strip down the middle of the omelet and flip the sides over the berries. Let cook until set. Split the omelet in half and serve, using the berry juice as a sauce. Add salt and pepper to taste.

YIELDS 2 SERVINGS; SERVING SIZE ½ OMELET

Calories: 200 | Carbohydrates: 8g | Fat: 12g | Sodium: 170mg | Fiber: 2g

The Vanilla Smoothie Breakfast

*This basic smoothie will become a favorite in your house!
Simple and delicious, it will fill you up with wheat bran
and provide calcium through the yogurt.*

INGREDIENTS

1 cup low-fat yogurt, plain

1 package sugar substitute

1 teaspoon pure vanilla extract

2 ice cubes

1 tablespoon wheat bran

Place all ingredients in the blender and blend until the ice cubes are pulverized.

SERVES 1

Calories: 180 | Carbohydrates: 21g | Fat: 4g | Sodium: 170mg | Fiber: 1g

Oatmeal-Walnut Bread

This quick and easy breakfast bread is excellent with eggs.
It also works well as an afternoon snack.

INGREDIENTS

2 eggs

1 cup milk

2 tablespoons melted unsalted
butter

2 tablespoons Splenda

1 teaspoon salt

1 teaspoon vanilla extract

1 teaspoon baking soda

1 teaspoon baking powder

1 teaspoon cinnamon

½ cup rice flour or tapioca flour

1 cup uncooked old-fashioned or
Irish oatmeal

1 cup walnut pieces, toasted

1. Preheat oven to 350°F. Prepare a standard bread loaf pan with non-stick spray. In a large bowl, beat the eggs, milk, butter, Splenda, salt, and vanilla extract together.

2. Stir in the rest of the ingredients and mix thoroughly.

3. Bake for 60 minutes on a rack in the middle of the oven. Remove the bread from oven and set on a cooling rack. Slice and serve warm or at room temperature.

YIELDS 1 LOAF;
SERVING SIZE 1 SLICE, 12 SLICES PER LOAF

Calories: 180 | Carbohydrates: 17g | Fat: 10g |
Sodium: 360mg | Fiber: 2g

Grilled Peaches with Cream Cheese

Lemon juice and cream cheese contrast refreshingly with sweet peaches, and the cinnamon adds a little jolt.

INGREDIENTS

4 large peaches, halved and pitted

4 teaspoons lemon juice

3 tablespoons cream cheese at room temperature

1 tablespoon Splenda

4 pinches cinnamon

1. Sprinkle the peaches with lemon juice.

2. Place the peaches cut-side down on grill over medium flame.

3. Grill peach halves for about 4 minutes. Meanwhile, combine cream cheese and Splenda. Turn the peaches and divide the cheese among the halves.

4. Let grill for another 2–3 minutes. Sprinkle with cinnamon and serve hot.

YIELDS 4 SERVINGS; SERVING SIZE 1 PEACH

Calories: 100 | Carbohydrates: 17g | Fat: 4g | Sodium: 30mg | Fiber: 3g

Multigrain Pancakes

You can omit the soy or rice milk in this recipe and increase the orange and apple juices, if you'd like.

INGREDIENTS

1 cup whole-wheat flour

½ cup all-purpose flour

¼ cup rye flour

¼ cup cornmeal

1 teaspoon baking powder

¼ cup brown sugar

½ teaspoon salt

1 teaspoon cinnamon

2 teaspoons vanilla

1 ripe banana

½ cup soy milk or rice milk

½ cup orange juice

½ cup apple juice

Vegetable oil

Make Breakfast Fun

Any pancake becomes extra yummy if you make it a teddy bear pancake. On the griddle, beside the round pancake, pour out two dots for eyes and a swirl for a smile. Assemble and see smiles of your own. Grrrr-eat!

1. In large bowl, combine flours, cornmeal, baking powder, brown sugar, salt, and cinnamon; mix well with wire whisk.

2. In blender or food processor, combine vanilla, banana, and soy or rice milk; blend until smooth. Add orange and apple juices; blend until smooth again.

3. Add liquid mixture all at once to dry ingredients; mix with wire whisk until blended. Let batter stand for 15 minutes.

4. Heat large nonstick skillet over medium heat. Brush oil over surface. Pour batter onto skillet ¼ cup at a time. Cook until edges appear dry and bubbles form and just start to break on the surface. Gently turn pancakes and cook on second side until done.

SERVES 6

Calories: 230 | Carbohydrates: 51g | Fat: 1g | Sodium: 290mg | Fiber: 5g

Egg and Veggie Scramble

Use your favorite vegetables in this easy breakfast recipe.

INGREDIENTS

2 tablespoons olive oil

½ cup chopped onion

1 cup sliced mushrooms

½ cup chopped red bell pepper

¼ teaspoon salt

⅛ teaspoon pepper

½ teaspoon dried thyme leaves

8 eggs

2 tablespoons water

½ cup grated, dairy-free soy cheese

1. In large skillet, heat olive oil over medium heat. Add onion, mushrooms, and red bell pepper; cook and stir 4–5 minutes, or until vegetables are tender. Sprinkle with salt, pepper, and thyme leaves.

2. Meanwhile, in medium bowl combine eggs and water and beat until frothy. Add to skillet when vegetables are tender. Cook, stirring occasionally, until eggs are just set but still moist.

3. Sprinkle with cheese, remove from heat, and cover. Let stand 3–4 minutes, or until cheese melts. Serve immediately.

SERVES 4

Calories: 270 | Carbohydrates: 6g | Fat: 18g | Sodium: 530mg | Fiber: <1g

Bacon Eggs Benedict

You can make the sauce, rice cakes, and bacon ahead of time. When you want to eat, cook the Egg-Free Scrambled Eggs, assemble the dish, and broil until hot.

INGREDIENTS

¾ cup short-grain rice

1 egg

½ teaspoon dried basil leaves

¼ teaspoon salt

1 tablespoon olive oil

4 slices gluten-free bacon

1 recipe Egg-Free Scrambled "Eggs" (page 43)

1 cup rice or soy milk

2 tablespoons cornstarch or superfine rice flour

¼ teaspoon salt

½ cup shredded, dairy-free soy cheese

Is it Overdoing Things to Put a Lot of Time into a Child's Breakfast Preparation?

Preparing a good breakfast can be stressful, but there is no better way to start your child's day, not only blood-sugar wise, but for energy, concentration, and even happiness. A good start is worth the time.

1. In medium saucepan, cook rice according to package directions for sticky rice. Cool completely. When cold, beat in egg, basil leaves, and ¼ teaspoon salt. Form mixture into 6 cakes. Heat olive oil in a medium saucepan. Pan-fry cakes on both sides for 4–6 minutes per side, until golden brown. Remove from pan.

2. Cook bacon until crisp, crumble, and set aside. Prepare Egg-Free Scrambled "Eggs." In a microwave-safe measuring cup, combine rice or soy milk with cornstarch or rice flour and ¼ teaspoon salt. Microwave on high 1–2 minutes, stirring once with wire whisk during cooking time, until thick. Stir in cheese until melted.

3. Preheat broiler. Place rice cakes on a broiler pan. Top with crumbled bacon, some of the Egg-Free Scrambled "Eggs," and the cheese sauce. Broil 6" from heat source until food is hot and the top starts to brown and bubble. Serve.

SERVES 6

Calories: 418 | Carbohydrates: 25g | Fat: 25g | Sodium: 902 mg

Eggless French Toast

Serve this French toast hot from the griddle with some whipped honey and fresh raspberries.

INGREDIENTS

1 ripe banana, mashed

1 tablespoon lemon juice

⅓ cup vanilla rice milk

½ teaspoon cinnamon

1 tablespoon sugar

Dash salt

1 teaspoon gluten-free vanilla

4 slices day-old, gluten-free bread

1 tablespoon vegetable oil

1. In blender or food processor, combine all ingredients except bread and oil; blend or process until smooth. Pour into shallow bowl.

2. Soak bread in mixture 2–3 minutes. Heat vegetable oil in a large skillet over medium heat. Cook bread in skillet, turning once, until golden brown on both sides and slightly puffy, about 4–6 minutes. Serve immediately.

SERVES 4

Calories: 220 | Carbohydrates: 33g | Fat: 10g | Sodium: 55mg | Fiber: 2g

Egg-Free Scrambled "Eggs"

Turmeric is an inexpensive spice that adds a golden color to these "eggs."
It is also a good source of antioxidants.

INGREDIENTS

2 tablespoons olive oil

1 cup sliced mushrooms

½ cup chopped onion

2 cloves garlic, minced

½ teaspoon salt

⅛ teaspoon pepper

1 (8-ounce) block medium-firm
    tofu, crumbled

1 tablespoon water

½ teaspoon turmeric

1 cup shredded, nondairy vegan
    soy cheese

1. Heat olive oil in large skillet over medium heat. Add mushrooms, onion, and garlic; cook and stir until tender, about 6 minutes. Sprinkle with salt and pepper.

2. Add crumbled tofu to skillet. In small bowl, combine water and turmeric; mix well. Sprinkle evenly over tofu. Cook and stir until heated and most of the moisture has been absorbed.

3. Sprinkle with cheese, cover, remove from heat, and let stand 2–3 minutes to melt cheese. Serve immediately.

They Won't Know What They're Missing

Kids know what they live. If you start them early on eggless "eggs," they will come to enjoy the taste and texture and not even miss the real thing.

SERVES 4

Calories: 220 | Carbohydrates: 7g | Fat: 14g | Sodium: 780mg | Fiber: 1g

Chicken and Apple Patties

*Rather than feed your kids sausages full of nitrates, try this easy recipe.
It's flavorful and good for you, too.*

INGREDIENTS

2 tablespoons olive oil

1 onion, finely chopped

3 cloves garlic, minced

1 cup finely chopped, peeled
   apple

1 tablespoon brown sugar

2 tablespoons lemon juice

1½ pounds gluten-free ground
   chicken

1 teaspoon salt

¼ teaspoon white pepper

1 teaspoon dried thyme leaves

1. In large saucepan, heat olive oil over medium heat. Add onion and garlic; cook and stir until tender, about 5 minutes. Remove from heat and add apple, brown sugar, and lemon juice. Let cool for 20 minutes.

2. Transfer cooled mixture to large bowl and add chicken, salt, pepper, and thyme leaves; work with your hands until combined.

3. Form mixture into 16 patties. You can freeze the patties at this point, or cook them in more olive oil, turning once, until thoroughly cooked, about 3–4 minutes per side. To cook frozen patties, let thaw in refrigerator overnight, then proceed as directed.

SERVES 8

Calories: 170 | Carbohydrates: 6g | Fat: 10g |
Sodium: 340mg | Fiber: <1g

Cinnamon French Toast

*Purchased gluten-free bread can be dense and rather stiff
perfect for making the best French toast.*

INGREDIENTS

¼ cup orange juice

¼ cup rice milk

1 ripe banana

2 tablespoons sugar

½ teaspoon cinnamon

⅛ teaspoon cardamom

1 teaspoon gluten-free vanilla

¼ teaspoon salt

6 slices day-old gluten-free, dairy-
free bread

1 tablespoon vegetable oil

1. In food processor or blender, combine orange juice, rice milk, and banana and blend until smooth. Pour into a shallow bowl and stir in sugar, cinnamon, cardamom, vanilla, and salt; mix well.

2. Soak bread in mixture for 2–3 minutes. Heat vegetable oil in a large skillet over medium heat. Cook bread in skillet, turning once, until golden brown on both sides and slightly puffy, about 4–6 minutes. Serve immediately.

SERVES 6

Calories: 210 | Carbohydrates: 31g | Fat: 9g |
Sodium: 110mg | Fiber: 2g

Save Some for Later

French toast freezes beautifully. Cook according to the recipe, then cool for 15 minutes on a wire rack. Place on a cookie sheet and freeze until hard. Then package into hard-sided containers, label, seal, and freeze up to 3 months. To use, pop into a toaster or toaster oven right from the freezer for 4–7 minutes.

Crunchy Coffee Cake

Raisins, chocolate chips, dried cranberries, or chopped nuts (if you're not allergic) could be used in place of the dried cherries if you'd like.

INGREDIENTS

1 cup butter, softened

1 cup brown sugar

1 cup sour cream

2 teaspoons gluten-free vanilla

2 eggs

2 egg whites

2 tablespoons lemon juice

2½ cups Gluten-Free, Soy-Free Baking Mix (page 47)

1 teaspoon cinnamon

1½ cups Spicy and Sweet Granola (page 48)

½ cup dried chopped cherries

1. Preheat oven to 350°F. Spray a 9" × 13" baking pan with nonstick gluten-free cooking spray and set aside. In large bowl, combine butter and sugar and beat until light and fluffy.

2. Add sour cream, vanilla, eggs, egg whites, and lemon juice; beat until blended. Add Baking Mix and cinnamon; mix just until blended.

3. Spread half of batter into prepared baking pan. Top with half of the granola, remaining batter, then remaining granola. Top with dried cherries.

4. Bake 35–40 minutes, or until cake is golden brown and springs back when lightly touched in center. Let cool completely on wire rack.

SERVES 16

Calories: 380 | Carbohydrates: 52g | Fat: 18g | Sodium: 39mg | Fiber: 6g

Gluten-Free, Soy-Free Baking Mix

If you're allergic to rice or soy, this is a good flour blend. Be sure to use potato-starch flour, not regular potato flour.

INGREDIENTS

1¼ cups millet flour

1 cup white sorghum flour

1 cup potato-starch flour

¾ cup coconut flour

1½ teaspoons xanthan gum

Combine all ingredients in medium bowl and mix well with wire whisk. Store covered, at room temperature, up to 2 weeks.

YIELDS 4 CUPS

Per cup:
Calories: 720 | Carbohydrates: 141g | Fat: 11g | Sodium: 0mg | Fiber: 41g

Spicy and Sweet Granola

You can add or subtract spices as you'd like in this excellent breakfast-cereal recipe. The oats can be omitted if you can't find those guaranteed gluten-free; just use more corn and rice cereal.

INGREDIENTS

4 cups gluten-free rolled oats

3 cups flaked rice cereal

2 cups gluten-free corn flakes

½ cup sesame seeds

1 cup honey

⅓ cup vegetable oil

¼ cup orange juice

1 cup brown sugar

2 teaspoons cinnamon

1 teaspoon ground ginger

½ teaspoon ground cardamom

2 teaspoons gluten-free vanilla extract

2 cups golden raisins

1 cup dried blueberries

1 cup dried cranberries

1. Preheat oven to 300°F. In large roasting pan, combine oats, flaked rice cereal, corn flakes, and sesame seeds and mix well.

2. In small saucepan, combine honey, vegetable oil, orange juice, brown sugar, cinnamon, ginger, and cardamom and mix well. Heat until warm, then remove from heat and stir in vanilla. Drizzle over cereal in roasting pan and toss to coat.

3. Bake 40–50 minutes; stirring twice, until cereals are glazed and toasted. Stir in dried fruits, then cool completely. When cool, break into pieces and store at room temperature in airtight container.

YIELDS 12 CUPS; 24 SERVINGS

Calories: 300 | Carbohydrates: 59g | Fat: 6g | Sodium: 45mg | Fiber: 4g

Gluten-Free Oats

Cross-contamination can be a big problem with most brands of commercial oatmeal. Even if the mill is dedicated only to oats, if the grains are planted in a field near wheat it can become polluted. There are some companies working on this. Gluten Free Oats and Chateau Cream Hill Estates both claim their oats are gluten-free.

School Lunch, Home Lunch, and Lunch on the Run

Ultimate Grilled Cheeseburger Sandwich

Eating a healthy diet doesn't always mean making sacrifices; it means making more intelligent choices about ingredients and portion sizes. Use an indoor grill to cook this sandwich, and top it with your favorite fixin's.

INGREDIENTS

1 tablespoon olive oil

1 teaspoon butter

2 thick slices of 7-grain bread

1 ounce Cheddar cheese

½ pound (8 ounces) 90% lean
    ground round

Optional seasonings to taste:

Worcestershire sauce

Fresh minced garlic

Balsamic vinegar

Toppings of your choice, such
    as stone-ground mustard,
    mayonnaise, and so on

The Olive Oil Factor

Once you've used an olive oil and butter mixture to butter the bread for a toasted or grilled sandwich, you'll never want to use just plain butter again. The olive oil helps make the bread crunchier and imparts a subtle taste difference to the sandwich as well.

1. Preheat your indoor grill. Combine the olive oil and butter, then use half of the mixture to butter one side of each slice of bread. Place the Cheddar cheese on the unbuttered side of 1 slice of bread and top with the other slice, buttered-side up.

2. Combine the ground round with the Worcestershire sauce, garlic, and balsamic vinegar, if using. Shape the ground round into a large, rectangular patty, a little larger than a slice of the bread. Grill the patty and then the cheese sandwich. (If you are using a large indoor grill, position the hamburger at the lower end, near the area where the fat drains; grill the cheese sandwich at the higher end.)

3. Once the cheese sandwich is done, separate the slices of bread, being careful not to burn yourself on the cheese. Top 1 slice with the hamburger and add your choice of condiments and fixin's.

SERVES 4

Calories: 210 | Carbohydrates: 8g | Fat: 13g | Sodium: 170mg | Fiber: 1g

Creamed Broccoli and Cheddar Soup

The broccoli-and-cheddar combination is totally classic and very tasty. You can purée the soup or leave it chunky; it's great either way.

INGREDIENTS

1 broccoli crown

1 tablespoon whole-wheat flour

2 tablespoons cold water

3½ cups chicken both

1 teaspoon basic mustard

1 teaspoon Splenda

Salt and freshly ground black pepper to taste

1 teaspoon fresh lemon zest

½ cup half-and-half

4 tablespoons grated sharp Vermont or Wisconsin Cheddar cheese

⅛ teaspoon ground nutmeg

¼ cup toasted pine nuts for garnish

1. Blanch the broccoli in boiling water for 3 minutes. Drain and cool under cold running water to set the color. When cool, chop and set aside.

2. Stir flour into water and combine to make a smooth paste.

3. In a soup pot, whisk together the broth, the flour paste, mustard, Splenda, salt, pepper, and lemon zest. Return the broccoli to the pot and heat, stirring. Add the half-and-half. Divide among 4 bowls.

4. Float the cheese and nutmeg on top and sprinkle with pine nuts.

YIELDS 4 SERVINGS; SERVING SIZE 8 OUNCES

Calories: 200 | Carbohydrates: 15g | Fat: 12g | Sodium: 460mg | Fiber: 5g

Soup's On!

Kids love soup. Make large batches of this yummy soup as a family project and then freeze it into individual servings by measuring out into freezer bags. They can be popped into the microwave for a warm, quick lunch. Simply warm them up in the bag, open the bag, and transfer into a bowl.

Tomato Bisque with Sour Cream

*Your dinner companions will think you've worked
all day on this fresh and delightful soup.*

INGREDIENTS

1 teaspoon butter or tub
    margarine, melted

1½ tablespoons potato flour

2 shallots, peeled

1 (13-ounce) can chicken broth

1 teaspoon Splenda

1 pint cherry tomatoes, stems
    removed

Salt and pepper to taste

1 teaspoon dried oregano

½ cup low-fat sour cream

Fresh chives, chopped for garnish

1. Put everything but the sour cream
   and garnish into your blender; purée.
   Transfer to a pot and bring to a boil.

2. Reduce heat and simmer for 10 minutes. Ladle into bowls and float sour
   cream on top. Sprinkle with chives
   and serve.

YIELDS 6 SERVINGS; SERVING SIZE 5 OUNCES

Calories: 110 | Carbohydrates: 19g | Fat: 3.5g |
Sodium: 125mg | Fiber: 1g

Read Your Labels

Yummy little garnishes and
snacks are often loaded with
sugar and trans fat. For
instance, Campbell's cream
soups are made with consider-
able amounts of sugar. Who
knew? That's why label reading
is so important. Take your
reading glasses with you to the
supermarket, and find brands
you can trust.

Marinated Chicken Tenders on Toothpicks

This marinade is both sweet and spicy with a nutty undertone from the sesame seed oil. These can be made on a grill or under the broiler. Make this to fill your family with energy in the form of protein.

INGREDIENTS

1 pound chicken tenders, cut in bite-sized pieces

18 wooden toothpicks, soaked for 20 minutes in warm water

1 tablespoon toasted sesame seed oil

½ cup orange juice, no sugar added

3 tablespoons tamari sauce

3 tablespoons chili sauce

1 teaspoon basic mustard

Toothpick Magic

Kids will eat just about anything on a toothpick! Dress these up with doilies on the plates and you'll see a nourishing meal devoured as if it were a play event.

1. Put one or two pieces of chicken tenders on each presoaked toothpick. In a bowl, whisk the rest of the ingredients together and coat each piece of chicken.

2. Cover the bowl and marinate, refrigerated, for at least 60 minutes, or up to 3 hours. Preheat broiler or grill to 400°F.

3. Grill or broil the chicken tenders for about 5 minutes per side, depending on the thickness. Turn them often until nicely browned.

**SERVES 6 AS A SNACK;
SERVING SIZE 2–3 TENDERS**

Calories: 120 | Carbohydrates: 5g | Fat: 3.5g | Sodium: 1020mg | Fiber: 0g

Tasty Tuna Melt

*For a fun change, bake a potato in the microwave,
slice it open and spread it out, top it with tuna and cheese,
and bake again until bubbly. You will have a tuna melt potato!*

INGREDIENTS

2 English muffins or bagels, split
in half

1 (6-ounce) can chunk tuna in
water

2 tablespoons mayonnaise

¼ cup shredded or sliced cheese:
Mozzarella, Cheddar, or
American

1. Preheat the oven to 350°F.

2. Place English muffin or bagel halves
onto a cookie sheet or a sheet of
aluminum foil.

3. Use the can opener to open the
tuna, then carefully drain the water.

4. In a small bowl, combine the
drained tuna with the mayonnaise.
Mix well.

5. Top each English muffin or bagel
half with tuna, then with the cheese.

6. Bake 5–8 minutes, or until the
cheese is melted.

MAKES 4 TUNA MELT SANDWICH HALVES

Per half:
Calories: 190 | Carbohydrates: 13g | Fat: 9g |
Sodium: 360mg | Fiber: <1g

Cheesy Apple Melts

This crunchy and cheesy sandwich melt is just delicious.
Keep the spread in the refrigerator for up to 3 days.

INGREDIENTS

1 apple, diced

½ cup chopped celery

1 tablespoon lemon juice

⅓ cup mayonnaise

½ cup chopped red onion

1 cup diced dairy-free, vegan
 Cheddar cheese

¼ cup shredded dairy-free vegan
 Parmesan cheese

8 slices French bread

2 tablespoons olive oil

1. In small bowl, combine all ingredients except bread and olive oil. Mix well.

2. Slice the bread on an angle to make larger slices. Make sandwiches with the filling. Brush outsides of sandwiches with olive oil. Cook in covered preheated skillet 5–7 minutes, turning once, until bread is crisp and golden and filling is hot. Serve immediately.

SERVES 4

Calories: 670 | Carbohydrates: 78g | Fat: 30g |
Sodium: 1610mg | Fiber: 8g

How Do I Get My Child to Try Unusual Foods?

Kids like basics, to be sure. But by involving them in the process (from shopping to preparing), you'll lure them into trying—and usually liking—new ideas. And of course, having other family members eating—and saying how delicious—the new foods are can't hurt either!

Turkey Wraps

*These flavorful wrap sandwiches are really delicious.
If you like your food spicy, add another jalapeño or two.*

INGREDIENTS

1 tablespoon olive oil

½ cup chopped red onion

1 red bell pepper, chopped

1 jalapeño pepper, minced

2 cups cubed cooked turkey

1 tablespoon lemon juice

2 tablespoons chopped flat-leaf parsley

6 (8-inch) corn tortillas

2 (3-ounce) packages dairy-free vegan cream cheese, softened

1 cup baby spinach leaves

Use Those Leftovers

When you roast a turkey for Thanksgiving or other holidays, remove the meat within 2 days. Chop or dice, then package into hard-sided freezer containers. Label, seal, and freeze up to 3 months. To use, let stand in refrigerator overnight, then use in recipes from casseroles to sandwich spreads. Use the bones to make stock.

1. In medium saucepan, heat olive oil over medium heat. Add red onion; cook and stir 2 minutes. Add bell pepper and jalapeño pepper; cook and stir 3—4 minutes longer.

2. Remove from heat and stir in turkey, lemon juice, and parsley.

3. Soften tortillas as directed on package. Arrange on work surface; spread each with 1 ounce of the cream cheese. Layer spinach leaves on top of the cream cheese. Top with turkey mixture, divided among the tortillas.

4. Roll up the tortillas, enclosing filling. Cut in half. Serve immediately.

SERVES 6

Calories: 220 | Carbohydrates: 21g | Fat: 8g | Sodium: 130mg | Fiber: 3g

Chicken Lettuce Wraps

These simple sandwiches can be prepared in minutes, if you use the shredded carrots you can buy in the produce aisle at your grocery store.

INGREDIENTS

1 (7-ounce) jar roasted red peppers

2 cups chopped cooked chicken

½ cup eggless mayonnaise

½ teaspoon dried basil leaves

¼ cup chopped green onions

½ cup shredded carrots

4–6 large lettuce leaves

1. Drain peppers on paper towel and chop into small pieces. In medium bowl, combine peppers with chicken, mayonnaise, basil, green onions, and carrots.

2. Spread this mixture on lettuce leaves; roll up. Serve immediately.

SERVES 4

Calories: 250 | Carbohydrates: 16g | Fat: 8g | Sodium: 700mg | Fiber: <1g

Tuna and Apple Crunch Sandwich

*A sweet crunch will make your tuna salad sandwich so much tastier. If you
don't have an apple for this recipe, try a chopped pear.*

INGREDIENTS

1 (6-ounce) can chunk tuna in
  water

1 small apple

1 tablespoon mayonnaise

1 pita pocket, cut in half

Normal Is Boring

Okay, so a kid does not think of
putting apple in a tuna sandwich, but you can show your
child, and they can show their
friends, that when it comes to
food, normal is boring. You'll
be surprised at how much they
enjoy mixing things up a bit
when you offer it.

1. Use the can opener to open the
   tuna, then carefully drain the water
   out.

2. Peel, core, and chop apple.

3. Combine the tuna, apple, and mayonnaise in a medium bowl. Mix well.

4. Cut pita pocket in half, open up
   both sides, and stuff half the mixture in each pocket.

MAKES 2 TUNA SANDWICHES

Calories: 460 | Carbohydrates: 28g | Fat: 13g |
Sodium: 1050mg | Fiber: 3g

Chicken à la King Wraps

Instead of serving over biscuits,
make your next Chicken à la King into a wrap sandwich!

INGREDIENTS

1 tablespoon olive oil

1 cup sliced mushrooms

1 green bell pepper, chopped

2 cups chopped Poached Chicken
   (page 76)

½ teaspoon salt

⅛ teaspoon pepper

½ teaspoon dried marjoram leaves

2 tablespoons diced pimiento

2 tablespoons cornstarch

⅔ cup rice milk

4 (6-inch) corn tortillas

1. In medium skillet, heat olive oil over medium heat. Add mushrooms and bell pepper; cook and stir until tender, about 5 minutes. Add chicken, salt, pepper, marjoram, and pimento; cook 3 minutes.

2. In small bowl, combine cornstarch and rice milk and mix well. Add to skillet; cook and stir until sauce thickens, about 3–5 minutes. Make wrap sandwiches with the tortillas. Serve immediately.

SERVES 4

Calories: 240 | Carbohydrates: 22g | Fat: 12g | Sodium: 400mg | Fiber: 3g

Reign of the (à la) King

The origins of Chicken à la King are murky. It was invented a long time ago, but could have been at the Brighton Beach Hotel in New York City or Claridge's in London. It is made of chicken, mushrooms, pimentos, and green peppers in a cream sauce flavored with sherry, usually served on toast. There are many variations of it, but not as a sandwich, until now!

Sautéed Sausage and Peppers

It's easy to multiply this recipe for a small dinner for two to a group gathering.

INGREDIENTS

2 tablespoons olive oil, divided

5 ounces Italian sausage links

½ cup trimmed, seeded, and chopped red bell pepper

¼ cup chopped onion

½ cup chopped zucchini

Salt and freshly ground black pepper to taste

Organics at Your Fingertips

Finding organic foods is a snap (or click). The website *www .wholefoodsmarket.com* is a good source for organic home and dry goods. The best organic produce is still purchased through your local farmers' market.

1. In a small sauté pan, heat 1 tablespoon of the olive oil on medium-high. Place the sausage in the pan: it should sizzle on contact. (If not, remove the sausage immediately and let the pan heat to the proper temperature.) Let the sausage cook to a medium golden-brown color, turning as needed. Remove the sausage from the pan set aside, and keep warm.

2. Add the remaining olive oil to the sauté pan, and add the red pepper, onion, and zucchini. Sauté, uncovered, stirring until the vegetables have softened and start to caramelize a bit; remove from heat. Sprinkle with salt and pepper and toss.

3. To serve, cut the sausage links on a bias into thirds and place on a plate. Place the sautéed vegetables on top of the sausage. Serve immediately.

SERVES 1

Calories: 500 | Carbohydrates: 14g | Fat: 39g | Sodium: 820mg | Fiber: 3g

Broccoli Bacon Salad

*You can substitute frozen chopped broccoli,
cooked according to package directions, if you are in a time pinch.*

INGREDIENTS

2 bunches broccoli, chopped,
  cooked crisp-tender, drained

8 bacon strips, cooked and
  crumbled

1½ cups shredded Cheddar
  cheese

1 medium-size red onion,
  chopped

¼ cup red wine vinegar

2 tablespoons honey

¾ cup mayonnaise

1 tablespoon fresh lemon juice

1 teaspoon salt

½ teaspoon freshly ground black
  pepper

1. In a large bowl, combine the cooled broccoli, bacon, cheese, and onion.

2. Prepare the dressing by whisking together all the remaining ingredients. Pour the dressing over the broccoli mixture and toss to combine. Cover and refrigerate until ready to use.

SERVES 12

Calories: 230 | Carbohydrates: 11g | Fat: 18g |
Sodium: 490mg | Fiber: 3g

Shrimp Salad

Simple and satisfying.
Serve on a bed of baby spinach leaves with a light vinaigrette dressing.

INGREDIENTS

1 pound small shrimp, peeled and cooked

1 hard-boiled egg, chopped

1½ tablespoons chopped celery

1½ tablespoons chopped dill pickle

2 tablespoons thinly sliced shallots

2 tablespoons chopped yellow onion

2 tablespoons mayonnaise

1 teaspoon Dijon mustard

Salt and freshly ground black pepper to taste

1 tablespoon paprika

1. Combine the shrimp, egg, celery, pickle, shallots, and onion in a large bowl.

2. Mix the mayonnaise and mustard together in a small bowl. Add the mayonnaise mixture to the shrimp and toss to coat. Salt and pepper to taste and garnish with paprika.

SERVES 6

Calories: 130 | Carbohydrates: 1g | Fat: 6g | Sodium: 260mg | Fiber: 0g

Shrimp for the Shrimps

Kids love the sweet but tame taste of shrimp as a seafood choice. Make it a regular part of their food choices.

Layered Taco Salad

Add cooked chicken or ground beef to make this an even better-tasting entrée luncheon salad.

INGREDIENTS

½ cup mayonnaise

1 cup sour cream

½ teaspoon chili powder

½ teaspoon onion powder

½ teaspoon cumin

½ teaspoon garlic powder

1 teaspoon salt

1 teaspoon black pepper

¼ teaspoon red pepper flakes

4 cups shredded lettuce

8 ounces Cheddar cheese, shredded

8 ounces Swiss cheese, shredded

2 ripe tomatoes, finely chopped

1 (3½-ounce) can chopped ripe black olives

½ small bunch green onions, finely chopped

Salsa for garnish

1. In a medium-size mixing bowl, combine the mayonnaise, sour cream, chili powder, onion powder, cumin, garlic powder, salt, pepper, and red pepper flakes; whisk together until well blended.

2. Spread evenly on a serving platter with high sides. Top with the shredded lettuce, then the cheeses, then the tomatoes, black olives, and last, the green onion.

3. Cover and refrigerate overnight. Serve with a little salsa on the side.

SERVES 4

Calories: 840 | Carbohydrates: 16g | Fat: 73g | Sodium: 1440mg | Fiber: 2g

Microwave Meatloaf GF

Making meatloaf in the microwave is fun and easy.
You can flavor this basic recipe any way you'd like.

INGREDIENTS

3 slices gluten-free bacon

½ cup gluten-free tomato sauce, divided

2 tablespoons gluten-free apple cider vinegar

2 tablespoons brown sugar

1 tablespoon gluten-free mustard

½ cup cooked rice

¼ cup minced green onion

¼ teaspoon salt

⅛ teaspoon pepper

½ teaspoon dried basil leaves

1 pound gluten-free ground beef

King of the Leftovers

Meatloaf has great staying power and freezes easily. Make a few batches along with your child and then freeze them for future meals and sandwiches

1. Place bacon on microwave-safe plate and top with a paper towel. Microwave on 100% power 4 minutes, then rotate and microwave 1–2 minutes longer. Let bacon stand 2 minutes; drain and crumble.

2. In medium bowl, combine crumbled bacon with ¼ cup of the tomato sauce, vinegar, brown sugar, and mustard; mix well. Add rice, green onion, salt, pepper, and basil; stir. Let stand 10 minutes; add beef. Mix with hands until combined.

3. Form into a loaf and place in a 1½-quart microwave-safe dish. Microwave on high 10 minutes. Carefully drain off fat. Return dish to microwave and cook on high 5–7 minutes longer, until internal temperature registers 160°F.

4. Remove from microwave, cover with foil, and let stand on solid surface 5 minutes. Slice and serve.

SERVES 4

Calories: 290 | Carbohydrates: 15g | Fat: 14g | Sodium: 540mg | Fiber: <1g

Best Cookie Bars **GF**

These delicious bars are rich and decadent and take about 5 minutes to put together. They're perfect for packing into lunchboxes or filling a cookie jar.

INGREDIENTS

Unsalted butter (for greasing)

1 cup coconut

1 cup gluten-free white chocolate chips

1 cup special dark, gluten-free chocolate chips

1 cup chopped salted cashews

1 cup chopped pecans

1 (14-ounce) can gluten-free sweetened condensed milk

3 tablespoons gluten-free cocoa powder

1 teaspoon gluten-free vanilla flavoring

Read Closely for Gluten

When baking for kids who are allergic to gluten, be sure to read every single label on everything you buy. Some chocolates and even some canned milks can contain gluten. Look for mention of any type of flour or gluten, including wheat, rye, barley, wheat germ, couscous, seitan, or cereal extract.

1. Preheat oven to 325°F. Line a 13" × 9" baking pan with parchment paper; lightly grease with unsalted butter.

2. Layer coconut, white chocolate chips, dark chocolate chips, cashews, and pecans in pan in that order. In small bowl, combine condensed milk, cocoa powder, and vanilla; mix with wire whisk until blended. Drizzle this mixture evenly over ingredients in pan.

3. Bake 22–26 minutes, or until the bars are set and are bubbly all over the surface. Cool completely in pan. Then remove the bars along with the parchment paper from pan, peel off paper, and cut into bars. Store tightly covered at room temperature.

YIELDS 36 BARS

Calories: 160 | Carbohydrates: 1/g | Fat: 9g | Sodium: 55mg | Fiber: <1g

Avocado with Tuna Salad

A great entrée salad luncheon dish.
You can also serve the tuna salad in Boston lettuce leaf wraps.
And kids don't even know they love avocado, so let them find out!

INGREDIENTS

3 ounces albacore tuna, flaked

2 tablespoons mayonnaise

1 teaspoon Dijon mustard

1 hard-boiled egg, chopped

½ scallion bulb, minced

1 teaspoon chopped fresh dill

Salt and freshly ground black
    pepper to taste

¼ cup extra-virgin olive oil

2 tablespoons red wine vinegar

½ cup mixed greens

½ avocado

3 black olives, quartered, for
    garnish

1 pickle, sliced, for garnish

1. In a mixing bowl, mix together the tuna, mayonnaise, Dijon, egg, scallion, dill, salt, and pepper.

2. In another small bowl, whisk together the olive oil and vinegar; season with salt and pepper.

3. Toss the mixed greens with the vinaigrette; place on plate. Slice the avocado and fan it across the dressed greens. Top with the tuna salad. Garnish with the black olives and pickle.

SERVES 1

Calories: 1040 | Carbohydrates: 12g | Fat: 98g |
Sodium: 1260mg | Fiber: 9g

CHAPTER 6

Delightful Dinners for Everyone

Italian Ground Turkey Casserole

The extra mushrooms in this recipe replace some of the meat and add to the great flavor of this dish. It's reminiscent of lasagna, but because vegetables replace the pasta, it's much lower in calories.

INGREDIENTS

1 pound ground turkey (or turkey sausage, if preferred)

1 large onion, chopped

2 cups sliced fresh mushrooms

1 teaspoon minced garlic

1 teaspoon dried basil

¼ teaspoon dried oregano

½ teaspoon dried parsley

6 cups shredded cabbage

2 cups nonfat cottage cheese

⅛ cup Ener-G potato flour

4 ounces Parmesan cheese, grated (to yield 1 cup)

4 ounces part-skim mozzarella cheese, grated (to yield 1 cup)

1 (10.75-ounce) can condensed tomato soup

1 (6-ounce) can salt-free tomato paste

1 (16-ounce) can salt-free diced tomatoes

1. Place the ground turkey in a large covered skillet over medium-low heat and allow it to steam, being careful not to brown the meat. Drain off the grease and use paper towels to blot the meat to absorb any excess fat from the turkey. Add the onion, mushrooms, minced garlic, and herbs; toss lightly. Return the cover to the skillet and steam the vegetables until they are tender, about 3 minutes. Set aside.

2. Put the shredded cabbage in a large covered microwave-safe dish and steam until the cabbage is crisp-tender, about 5 minutes. (If your microwave doesn't have a carousel, turn the dish about halfway through the cooking time.) Drain the cabbage in a colander, being careful not to burn yourself from the steam. Press out any excess moisture.

3. Mix the cottage cheese, potato flour, and ½ of the Parmesan and mozzarella cheeses together. (Note: The potato flour acts as a bonding agent to keep the whey from separating

Italian Ground Turkey Casserole

(continued)

Kicking it Up a Notch

One of the easiest ways to add rich flavor to the condensed soup or casserole recipes without adding extra calories is to use ⅛ to ¼ teaspoon of Minor's bases, like Roasted Mirepoix, Onion, or Garlic.

from the cottage cheese. The traditional method of doing this is to add egg, but potato flour accomplishes the same thing without adding fat.) Add the condensed tomato soup, tomato paste, and canned tomatoes to the meat mixture; stir well.

4. Preheat oven to 350°F. Coat a deep rectangular baking dish or roasting pan with nonstick spray. Spoon ⅓ of the meat mixture into the bottom of the pan. Top with ½ of the cooked cabbage. Add another ⅓ of the meat mixture. Top with the remaining ½ of the cooked cabbage. Top that with the cottage cheese mixture. Add the remaining meat mixture and sprinkle the top of the casserole with the remaining Parmesan and mozzarella cheeses.

5. Bake for 45 minutes, or until the casserole is heated through and the cheeses on top are melted and bubbling.

SERVES 8

Calories: 310 | Carbohydrates: 23g | Fat: 12g | Sodium: 820mg | Fiber: 4g

Chicken Pasta with Herb Sauce

Once the sauce is heated, season it to taste.
Another option would be to use a commercial brand of low-fat
and low-sodium cream of chicken with herbs condensed soup.

INGREDIENTS

1 (10.5-ounce) can condensed
   cream of chicken soup

¼ cup skim milk

½ teaspoon Worcestershire sauce

1 teaspoon real mayonnaise

¼ cup grated Parmesan cheese

¼ teaspoon chili powder

½ teaspoon garlic powder

¼ teaspoon dried rosemary

¼ teaspoon dried thyme

¼ teaspoon dried marjoram

1 cup sliced mushrooms, steamed

½ pound (8 ounces) cooked,
   chopped chicken

4 cups cooked pasta

Freshly ground black pepper
   (optional)

1. Combine the soup, milk, Worcestershire, mayonnaise, and cheese in a saucepan; bring to a boil.

2. Reduce heat and add the chili powder, garlic powder, rosemary, thyme, and marjoram; stir well.

3. Add the mushrooms and chicken; simmer until heated through.

4. Serve over pasta and top with freshly ground pepper, if desired.

SERVES 4

Calories: 400 | Carbohydrates: 47g | Fat: 10g | Sodium: 720mg | Fiber: 3g

Turkey Meat Loaf with Thanksgiving Herbs

Meat loaf is a creative way to include vegetables in your children's meals. Even grownups who refuse to eat vegetables will eat them and love them in this recipe.

INGREDIENTS

2 tablespoons olive oil

1 yellow onion, minced

1 clove garlic, minced

1 large carrot, peeled and grated

1 zucchini, grated

1 stalk celery, chopped finely

1 cup corn bread stuffing (or any other stuffing you have premade)

1 cup chicken broth

2 eggs, beaten

1 teaspoon tomato paste

1 teaspoon Worcestershire sauce

¼ teaspoon ground cloves

1 teaspoon dried thyme

1 teaspoon dried sage leaves

Salt and pepper to taste

1 pound ground turkey

1. Heat oven to 350°F. Prepare a loaf pan with nonstick spray.

2. Heat the olive oil in a large frying pan; add the onion, garlic, carrot, zucchini, and celery. While the vegetables sauté, start soaking the corn bread stuffing in the chicken broth.

3. Mix the beaten eggs with the tomato paste, Worcestershire sauce, cloves, thyme, sage, salt, and pepper. (If the corn bread stuffing is seasoned, do not add salt.) Add the egg mixture to the vegetable mixture. Remove from heat. Cool slightly and stir in the soaked corn bread stuffing.

4. Stir the turkey into the egg-vegetable-stuffing mixture; mix well. Pour into the loaf pan. Bake for 1 hour.

SERVES 4

Calories: 390 | Carbohydrates: 18g | Fat: 23g | Sodium: 620mg | Fiber: 3g

Turkey Roll with Spinach and Cheese

You can use turkey in so many ways that your family will love. A grilled turkey leg and thigh is delicious on a summer night, as is this turkey roll. The finished design of a circle within a circle makes an attractive presentation.

INGREDIENTS

1½ pounds turkey breast, boneless and skinless

Salt and pepper to taste

1 (10-ounce) package spinach soufflé, thawed

1 tablespoon lemon juice

2 slices white American cheese, shredded

1 teaspoon olive oil

2 tablespoons Parmesan cheese, grated

2 slices bacon

You can also substitute vegetarian bacon for regular bacon and replace regular American cheese with low-fat American cheese.

1. Place the turkey breast between several sheets of waxed paper. Using a rubber hammer or meat mallet, flatten the turkey breast until it's about ½" thick. Sprinkle with salt and pepper.

2. Preheat the oven to 325°F. Spread the spinach on the turkey. Sprinkle with lemon juice, dot with shredded American cheese, and sprinkle with olive oil. Roll and skewer with metal poultry pins.

3. Sprinkle with Parmesan cheese. Wrap the top with bacon; roast until the internal temperature reaches 150°F. Let rest before carving.

Gobbling it Up

Turkey is such a great choice for a dinner main protein. By serving it in creative and interesting ways like this recipe, your child may never realize she is eating the same protein often.

SERVES 4

Calories: 370 | Carbohydrates: 7g | Fat: 14g | Sodium: 720mg | Fiber: <1g

Sunday Dinner Roasted Chicken

What could be more traditional than a family dinner of roast chicken with stuffing, gravy, and delicious vegetables? Stuffing the chicken with fruit and vegetables helps to lower your GI.

INGREDIENTS

2 tablespoons fresh rosemary leaves, or 1 tablespoon dried

½ lemon, skin and pulp, seeded and chopped

3-pound chicken, whole

Salt and pepper to taste

1 teaspoon olive oil

1 apple, peeled, cored, and chopped

1 medium red onion, chopped

½ fennel bulb, chopped

2 celery stalks, chopped

1 teaspoon thyme leaves

4 prunes, chopped

1 tablespoon orange peel

2 ounces walnuts, chopped

1 cup chicken broth

1. Mix the rosemary and lemon pulp; sprinkle the chicken with salt and pepper. Push the lemon and rosemary under the skin of the chicken, working it right down into the thigh.

2. Heat the olive oil and sauté the apple, onion, fennel, celery, thyme, prunes, and orange peel for 10 minutes. Add the walnuts at the end. When cool enough to handle, stuff the chicken with this mixture. Close the openings at neck and tail with small skewers.

3. Roast the chicken for 90 minutes at 350°F; baste every 15 minutes with the chicken broth.

SERVES 4

Calories: 910 | Carbohydrates: 21g | Fat: 65g | Sodium: 470mg | Fiber: 5g

Potatoes Sautéed in Olive Oil and Herbs

This is ideal for a family dinner, but it works just as well for two. You can eat half of it one night and the other half two days later. You can also use the leftover potatoes and herbs to make a great potato salad.

INGREDIENTS

8 large new or fingerling potatoes, scrubbed and sliced ¼" thick

2 tablespoons water

2 tablespoons olive oil

¼ cup fresh Italian flat-leaf parsley, chopped

2 teaspoons dried rosemary or 1 tablespoon fresh rosemary

1 teaspoon dried sage leaves or 1 tablespoon fresh sage leaves, torn

Salt and pepper to taste

1. Prepare a nonstick saucepan with nonstick spray. Add the potatoes and water; cover and cook for 15 minutes over medium heat.

2. Remove the lid. Toss the potatoes with olive oil, herbs, salt, and pepper. Reset heat to medium-high.

3. Brown quickly and serve.

YIELDS 4 SERVINGS; SERVING SIZE ⅔ CUP

Calories: 120 | Carbohydrates: 13g | Fat: 7g | Sodium: 360mg | Fiber: 2g

Finding a Good Balance

Don't cut back on side dishes to cut back on carbs. A well-balanced meal should be fun and interesting as well as healthy. It's all about balance, a lesson your child with diabetes will carry for a lifetime.

Kids' Favorite Meatloaf

*Actually, this is much loved
by grownups as well as children.*

INGREDIENTS

2 whole eggs

2 ½-inch-thick slices cornbread
(purchase premade at store or
use a mix)

¼ cup chili sauce

½ cup low-fat milk

½ teaspoon salt

¼ teaspoon pepper, or to taste

¼ cup grated Parmesan cheese

1 teaspoon dried oregano

1 pound ground meatloaf mix
(beef, pork, and veal) or 90%
lean beef

Optional: 1 slice sugar-free turkey
bacon or regular bacon

1. Preheat the oven too 325°F. Whirl
   everything but the meat and bacon
   in your blender.

2. Prepare a bread pan with nonstick
   spray. Pour the ingredients from the
   blender into a large bowl; add the
   meat. Mix thoroughly. Pile mixture
   into the bread pan without tamping
   it down.

3. Add bacon to the top, if that is your
   choice. Bake the meatloaf for 60
   minutes. Let cool slightly before
   cutting.

**YIELDS 16 ½-INCH SLICES (WHEN BAKED IN
STANDARD LOAF PAN MEASURING 4½" × 8½"
× 2½"); SERVING SIZE: ONE ½-INCH SLICE**

Calories: 90 | Carbohydrates: 5g | Fat: 4.5g |
Sodium: 220mg | Fiber: 0g

Poached Chicken

Poached chicken can be served on its own, diced up into broth or stock, or used in salads and sandwiches. It freezes well, too.

INGREDIENTS

1 tablespoon olive oil

1 onion, chopped

3 pounds chicken parts

2 carrots, sliced

3 cups water

½ teaspoon salt

1 bay leaf

½ teaspoon dried marjoram leaves

½ cup chopped celery leaves

What Is Poaching?

Poaching is a cooking technique whereby food is cooked in a liquid at a temperature just below a simmer. The French say that the liquid or broth is "smiling." It's important to carefully regulate the heat so the exterior of the meat doesn't overcook by the time the interior comes to a safe temperature.

1. In large soup pot, heat olive oil over medium heat. Add onion; cook and stir until onion starts to turn golden, about 8 minutes. Add chicken, skin-side down. Cook until browned, then turn chicken over.

2. Add all remaining ingredients to pot. Bring to a boil, then skim surface. Reduce heat to low, cover, and cook just below a simmer until chicken is thoroughly cooked, about 30–35 minutes. Remove chicken from liquid; let cool. Remove meat from bones; refrigerate or freeze.

3. The stock can be strained, then saved for soup.

SERVES 8

Calories: 350 | Carbohydrates: 4g | Fat: 21g | Sodium: 270mg | Fiber: 1g

Beef Piccata

*Piccata is usually made with chicken or veal,
but beef is a nice twist on a classic.*

INGREDIENTS

4 (6-ounce) top round steaks

3 tablespoons rice milk

2 tablespoons potato-starch flour

2 tablespoons cornstarch

½ teaspoon pepper

½ teaspoon salt

½ teaspoon paprika

2 tablespoons olive oil

1 (8-ounce) package mushrooms,
  sliced

3 cloves garlic, minced

1 cup beef stock

¼ cup dry red wine, if desired

3 tablespoons water

1 tablespoon cornstarch

1. Place beef between sheets of waxed paper and pound gently with meat mallet or rolling pin to slightly flatten. Place rice milk in a shallow bowl. In another shallow bowl, combine potato-starch flour, cornstarch, pepper, salt, and paprika.

2. Dip beef into milk, then into flour mixture to coat. In large saucepan, heat olive oil over medium-high heat. Add beef; brown on both sides, turning once, about 5–6 minutes. Remove from pan.

3. Add mushrooms and garlic to pan; cook and stir until tender, about 5–6 minutes. Add stock and wine and bring to a simmer. Return steaks to pan; simmer 15–25 minutes, or until beef is tender.

4. In small bowl, combine water and cornstarch; mix well. Add to saucepan; cook and stir until sauce is slightly thickened. Serve immediately.

SERVES 4

Calories: 360 | Carbohydrates: 14g | Fat: 14g |
Sodium: 690mg | Fiber: <1g

Grilled Salmon

Salmon is marinated for a while, then grilled to perfection in this delicious and easy recipe. Serve with roasted potatoes and steamed veggies.

INGREDIENTS

¼ cup orange juice

1 tablespoon lemon juice

2 tablespoons olive oil

1 tablespoon gluten-free Dijon mustard

2 cloves garlic, minced

½ teaspoon dried dill weed

4 (6-ounce) salmon steaks

Swimming Upstream Makes Them Yummy!

Salmon is so good for you. If you aren't allergic to this fish, try to eat it two times a week. It contains omega-3 fatty acids, an essential fatty acid that your body cannot make. The fats in salmon help lower the risk of heart disease, reduce cholesterol levels, reduce the symptoms of some autoimmune disorders such as rheumatoid arthritis and lupus, and reduce blood-clotting ability, which can help prevent heart attacks.

1. In 13" ⁄ 9" glass baking dish, combine orange juice, lemon juice, olive oil, mustard, garlic, and dill. Add salmon steaks; turn to coat. Cover and refrigerate 1–2 hours.

2. Prepare and preheat grill. Make sure grill is clean. Lightly oil the grill rack with vegetable oil. Add salmon; grill 6" from medium coals 9–12 minutes, turning once, until fish flakes easily when tested with fork. Discard remaining marinade.

SERVES 4

Calories: 270 | Carbohydrates: 3g | Fat: 13g | Sodium: 210mg | Fiber: 0g

Baby Back Ribs with Sauerkraut

Definitely a homestyle entrée.
This is a great dish for a casual family get-together.

INGREDIENTS

1 (32-ounce) container sauerkraut, drained and rinsed

3 cups shredded red cabbage

2 tablespoons plus 1 teaspoon paprika

4 cloves garlic, minced

1 (14½-ounce) can stewed tomatoes

3 pounds pork baby back ribs, trimmed of fat

Salt and freshly ground black pepper to taste

Messy Equals Yummy

Kids love meals they can eat with their hands, and they love feeling free to get messy doing so. Put out wet naps and bowls of lemon water and let your kids go nuts at this meal.

1. In a medium-size bowl, combine the sauerkraut, cabbage, 1 teaspoon of the paprika, garlic, and tomatoes; stir well to mix. Spread this mixture into the bottom of a large oiled baking dish.

2. Preheat oven to 375°.

3. Arrange the ribs on top of the sauerkraut mixture, curved-side up. Season with salt and pepper and the rest of the paprika. Bake in the oven, covered with foil, for about 1½ hours, or until the meat is tender. Uncover the pan, turn the ribs over, and bake for another 20 minutes (uncovered).

4. To serve, cut the ribs apart from the bones and serve over the sauerkraut.

SERVES 4

Calories: 640 | Carbohydrates: 23g | Fat: 29g | Sodium: 1170mg | Fiber: 9g

Veal Cutlets with Ricotta Cheese and Spinach

Ricotta is a rich fresh cheese, with 3.8 carbohydrates per ½ cup. It is slightly grainy, but smoother and a touch sweeter than cottage cheese.

INGREDIENTS

¾ pound veal scaloppini (pounded veal cutlets)

2 eggs beaten with a pinch of salt and pepper

2 tablespoons butter

10 ounces frozen chopped spinach, thawed, drained, and moisture squeezed out

2 cloves garlic, minced

Salt and pepper to taste

½ cup ricotta cheese

3 tablespoons sour cream

Pinch of freshly grated nutmeg

1 tablespoon freshly grated Parmesan cheese, plus extra for garnish

1. Soak the veal in the beaten egg for 30 minutes.

2. Melt the butter in a large sauté pan over medium-high heat; sauté the spinach and garlic, uncovered, for about 3–5 minutes. Season with salt and pepper. Remove the spinach from skillet and set aside.

3. Preheat the oven to 375°F.

4. In a large nonstick skillet over low heat, add ½ of the veal slices 1 at a time; cook just long enough to set the egg coating on both sides. Remove the slices as they are done and place in a 2-quart ovenproof casserole dish.

5. Put the ricotta and sour cream in a food processor (or a blender) with a pinch of nutmeg, salt and pepper, and the grated Parmesan; blend until smooth. Spread ½ of the cheese mixture over the veal with the back of a spoon. Layer ½ cup of the spinach on top.

Veal Cutlets with Ricotta Cheese and Spinach

(continued)

Thawing Spinach

Frozen chopped spinach and frozen cut-leaf spinach both contain a lot of water. If the recipe calls for draining the spinach, take time to do it properly or the recipe will be ruined. Thaw the spinach, then place it in a colander and squeeze with your hands. Then wrap the spinach in a kitchen towel and twist to remove the last bits of moisture.

6. Cook the rest of the scaloppini and layer it on top of the spinach in the casserole dish. Layer the other ½ cup spinach and spread the rest of the cheese on top. Bake for about 30 minutes, or until the cheese topping is set. Cut and serve like a lasagna, or scoop with a large spoon. Sprinkle a little Parmesan cheese on top to garnish.

SERVES 2

Calories: 800 | Carbohydrates: 13g | Fat: 60g | Sodium: 910mg | Fiber: 5g

Broiled Scallops with Apple-Wood Smoked Bacon

This is a delicious appetizer or first-course dish.
If serving as an appetizer, use skewers instead of toothpicks.

INGREDIENTS

6 slices of apple-wood smoked bacon, cut in half

12 large scallops, patted dry

1 tablespoon finely grated lemon zest

1 sprig fresh rosemary, finely minced

⅓ cup pitted and chopped black olives

2 plum tomatoes, peeled, seeded, and diced

2 tablespoons drained capers

1 clove garlic, chopped

2 tablespoons chopped fresh chives, divided

1 tablespoon extra-virgin olive oil

1. Preheat oven to 350°F.

2. Place the bacon on a nonstick baking sheet; precook for about 8 minutes. The bacon should be almost fully cooked but still pliable.

3. Drain the bacon on paper towels; discard the fat from the baking sheet.

4. Lay the bacon slices on a clean, flat work surface. Sprinkle the scallops with the lemon zest and rosemary; place 1 scallop on each piece of bacon. Wrap the bacon around the scallop and secure with a toothpick.

5. Place the olives, diced tomatoes, capers, garlic, and 1 tablespoon of the chives in a small mixing bowl.

6. Pour in enough olive oil to glaze the mixture together; mix to combine and adjust seasoning to taste. Set aside.

Broiled Scallops with Apple-Wood Smoked Bacon

(continued)

Sensational Scallops

Scallops are shellfish that are very low in fat. Sea scallops are the largest, followed by bay scallops, and then calico scallops. They should smell very fresh and slightly briny, like the sea. If they smell fishy, do not buy them. There may be a small muscle attached to the side of each scallop; pull it off and discard it because it can be tough.

7. Brush the wrapped scallops with the olive oil and either quickly brown under a preheated hot broiler or fry in a hot nonstick skillet for 1–2 minutes on each side, until slightly caramelized.

8. Remove the toothpick and serve the scallops with a dollop of the olive relish on the side. Sprinkle with the remaining chives.

SERVES 4

Calories: 140 | Carbohydrates: 4g | Fat: 9g | Sodium: 520mg | Fiber: 1g

Chicken Potpie Stew

A great do-ahead recipe for a group.
Easily prepared a day ahead and gently reheated just before serving.

INGREDIENTS

1 pound boneless, skinless chicken breasts

2 cups (or more, as needed) chicken stock

1 medium onion, diced

2 carrots, diced

2 stalks celery, diced

3 tablespoons arrowroot

½ cup evaporated skim milk

2 tablespoons chopped fresh parsley

1 tablespoon chopped fresh tarragon

Salt and freshly ground black pepper to taste

1. Rinse the chicken under cold running water and pat dry on paper towels. Trim the chicken of any fat, then cut into medium dice. Place the chicken in a medium-size saucepot and add the stock. The stock should just cover the chicken. Use more if needed. Bring the liquid to a gentle simmer; simmer until the chicken is just cooked. Remove the chicken with a slotted spoon and reserve.

2. Add the onions, carrots, and celery to the stock; cook at a simmer until the vegetables are tender. Dilute the arrowroot in the evaporated milk; add it to the stock and vegetables. Bring the stock to a full simmer to activate the arrowroot. Remove the pot from the heat and stir in the parsley, tarragon, and salt and pepper. Return the chicken to the sauce and simmer just to heat through. Serve in warm bowls.

SERVES 4

Calories: 250 | Carbohydrates: 22g | Fat: 3g |
Sodium: 330mg | Fiber: 3g

Pork Roast

The pork will continue to cook after you remove it from the oven,
adding an additional 5–8 degrees to the internal temperature.

INGREDIENTS

4-pound loin of pork, bone in

2 tablespoons extra-virgin olive oil

4 garlic cloves, sliced

2 sprigs fresh rosemary

1 bay leaf

1 cup dry white wine

Salt and freshly ground black
    pepper to taste

Green-Lighting Some Foods

While you want to teach your child about portion control, you also want them to feel some sense of freedom. With a main dish having a carb count as low as this one, allow your child to choose their portion size, small or large. Explain it's a healthy choice, green-light food.

1. Place the pork roast in a large plastic bag that can be sealed. Mix the oil, garlic, rosemary, bay leaf, wine, and salt and pepper in a small bowl until combined; add to the pork. Seal the bag; massage to ensure the pork is evenly coated with the marinade. Marinate for several hours in the refrigerator, turning occasionally.

2. Preheat oven to 450°F.

3. Place the loin in a roasting pan set on a rack. Season with more salt and pepper and baste the loin with the marinade. Roast for about 20 minutes, or until browned. Turn the heat down to 300°F and roast for another 45 minutes to 1 hour, or until the internal temperature reaches 150°F. Baste with the marinade while roasting.

4. Allow the pork to rest for at least 15 minutes before slicing. Serve slices on warm plates.

SERVES 6

Calories: 680 | Carbohydrates: 1g | Fat: 29g |
Sodium: 180mg | Fiber: 0g

Pizza with Goat Cheese and Vegetables

You can buy pizza dough from almost any supermarket, bakery, or pizza parlor. When you top the pizza with a good-quality sauce, extra veggies, and goat cheese, you have a marvelous lunch or supper.

INGREDIENTS

1 pound pizza dough

1 cup tomato sauce (from a jar or your own)

1 medium zucchini, sliced thinly

1 small onion, cut thinly

20 Greek or Italian olives, pitted and sliced

2 teaspoons olive oil

8 ounces goat cheese

1. Preheat oven to 475°F. Roll out the pizza dough to fit a 12" pan or pizza stone. Spread with sauce. Arrange the zucchini and onion over the sauce.

2. Sprinkle with olives and drizzle with olive oil. Dot the top with the cheese; bake for 15 minutes, or until the crust is brown, the cheese melts, and the topping bubbles.

Is it Okay to "Sneak" New Foods In?

Yes. Serve up meals like this pizza and call it something different, like White Pizza. In time, you can tell your child the ingredients (and they'll never say, "Eww! I won't try goat cheese!")

8 SLICES

Per Slice:

Calories: 310 | Carbohydrates: 32g | Fat: 14g | Sodium: 680mg | Fiber: 2g

Beef and Pea Stir-Fry

Two kinds of peas make this stir-fry special. Serve with hot cooked rice and a salad made with lettuce and mandarin oranges.

INGREDIENTS

1 pound boneless beef sirloin tip steak

⅓ cup beef stock

1 teaspoon sugar

2 tablespoons cornstarch

2 tablespoons apple juice

2 tablespoons soy sauce

⅛ teaspoon pepper

2 tablespoons olive oil

1 onion, sliced

2 cloves garlic, minced

2 cups snow peas, fresh or frozen

1 cup frozen baby peas, thawed and drained

1. Cut beef into ¼" × 4" strips against the grain. In medium bowl, combine stock, sugar, cornstarch, apple juice, soy sauce, and pepper; mix well. Add beef and let stand 15 minutes.

2. Drain beef, reserving marinade. Heat olive oil in wok or large skillet over medium-high heat. Add beef; stir-fry until browned, about 3–4 minutes. Remove beef from wok and set aside.

3. Add onion and garlic to wok; stir-fry 4–5 minutes, until crisp-tender. Add snow peas and baby peas to wok; stir-fry 2 minutes.

4. Stir marinade; add to wok along with beef. Stir-fry until sauce bubbles and thickens, about 4–5 minutes. Serve immediately over hot cooked rice.

SERVES 4

Calories: 370 | Carbohydrates: 22g | Fat: 19g | Sodium: 700mg | Fiber: 5g

Spaghetti Sauce

A combination of fresh and canned tomatoes creates a real depth of flavor in this simple recipe. Serve it with pasta. It freezes very well. And every kid should learn to make the family sauce.

INGREDIENTS

2 tablespoons olive oil

1 onion, chopped

3 cloves garlic, minced

1 cup chopped mushrooms

1 cup shredded carrots

2 (14-ounce) cans diced tomatoes, undrained

1 (6-ounce) can gluten-free tomato paste

6 plum tomatoes, chopped

1½ cups water

1 teaspoon dried basil leaves

½ teaspoon dried oregano leaves

½ teaspoon salt

¼ teaspoon pepper

1 bay leaf

1. Heat olive oil in large heavy saucepan; add onion and garlic and cook over medium heat until tender, 5–6 minutes. Add mushrooms and carrots; cook 4–5 minutes longer.

2. Add canned tomatoes, tomato paste, plum tomatoes, water, and remaining ingredients to saucepan. Bring to a boil, then reduce heat to low; cover pan and simmer 45–50 minutes, until sauce is blended and slightly thickened. Remove bay leaf and discard.

3. Serve immediately with cooked pasta, or cover and refrigerate up to 4 days. Freeze for longer storage.

YIELDS 1½ QUARTS; SERVING SIZE ½ CUP

Calories: 60 | Carbohydrates: 10g | Fat: 2.5g | Sodium: 240mg | Fiber: 3g

Sautéed Yellow Squash and Carrots

Kids love a palette that pleases their eyes as well as their taste buds. This side dish is a good example of a colorful recipe.

INGREDIENTS

2 tablespoons olive oil

2 shallots, minced

2 carrots, sliced

¼ cup water

3 yellow summer squash, sliced

½ teaspoon salt

⅛ teaspoon white pepper

½ teaspoon dried sage leaves

Know Your Squash

There are two basic kinds of squash: summer and winter. Summer squash are thin skinned and tender, cook quickly, and can be served raw. They include yellow squash and zucchini. Winter squash are hard, with thick shells, and they must be cooked before eating. Pumpkins, butternut squash, and acorn squash are included in this group.

1. In large saucepan, heat olive oil over medium heat. Add shallots; cook and stir 2 minutes. Add carrots; cook and stir 2 minutes. Add water; bring to a simmer. Cover saucepan; simmer 3 minutes.

2. Add squash; stir. Raise heat and simmer until liquid evaporates, stirring occasionally. Add salt, pepper, and sage leaves; cover, remove from heat, and let stand 3 minutes. Stir and serve.

SERVES 6

Calories: 90 | Carbohydrates: 11g | Fat: 4.5g | Sodium: 210mg | Fiber: 3g

CHAPTER 7

Holidays That Rock

Matzo Ball Soup

This traditional soup tastes best when made the day before serving. Gently reheat the matzo balls in a small amount of the soup before serving.

INGREDIENTS

Soup:

1 whole roasting chicken

3 whole carrots, cut into large chunks

4 celery sticks (stalks and tops), cut into large chunks

2 whole onions, quartered

½ cup chopped fresh parsley

1 parsnip, peeled and cut into large chunks

4 sprigs fresh dill

Salt and freshly ground black pepper to taste

1 tablespoon oil

Matzo balls:

3 large eggs, separated

2 tablespoons vegetable oil

½ cup matzo meal

1 teaspoon salt

2 tablespoons soup stock (from this recipe) or water

1. To prepare the soup: Use kitchen shears to cut the whole chicken into quarters. Place the chicken into a stockpot; fill the stockpot with water to cover chicken. Bring the stockpot to a boil. Skim off any impurities that rise to the top of the water. Add the rest of the ingredients for the soup. Reduce heat and let simmer, partially covered, for approximately 1½ hours, or until tender.

2. To prepare the matzo balls: Mix the egg yolks with the oil in a medium-size mixing bowl. Mix together the matzo meal, salt, and soup stock or water; add to the egg yolk mixture and stir to blend. Beat the egg whites to soft peaks. Fold the egg whites into the matzo mixture until just blended; refrigerate for 40 minutes. Remove from the refrigerator; make heaping tablespoon-size balls.

Matzo Ball Soup

(continued)

Be a Holiday Tradition Pioneer!

Holiday traditions can be yours and yours alone to start. Think about adding new recipes and treats that fit into a healthy diabetes lifestyle, but present it to your child as simply your own new and beloved family tradition. Watch it become one for your family for the ages.

3. Strain the soup, reserving the chicken for another use. Reserve the carrots. Put the strained soup back into the stockpot. Bring back to a low boil and carefully drop the matzo balls into the soup. Cover and simmer for about 40 minutes. Serve the matzo ball soup in warmed soup cups with a few slices of the reserved carrots.

SERVES 12

Calories: 330 | Carbohydrates: 12g | Fat: 21g | Sodium: 320mg | Fiber: 2g

Skewered Shrimp with Bacon

*This is an excellent appetizer or snack that older children
love almost as much as grownups do.*

INGREDIENTS

1 pound fresh or thawed frozen,
  raw shrimp (about 24 per
  pound)

¼ cup unsalted butter, melted

½ teaspoon garlic powder

Pepper to taste

8 strips of bacon, stretched, cut
  in thirds

1. Dip each shrimp in a combination of melted butter, garlic powder, and pepper.

2. Set broiler at 375°F. Wrap the shrimp with bacon and secure with presoaked wooden toothpicks.

3. Broil the shrimp until the bacon is cooked and the shrimps are pink, about 4–5 minutes per side.

**SERVES 6; SERVING SIZE 4 JUMBO SHRIMP
OR 6 EXTRA-LARGE SHRIMP**

Calories: 290 | Carbohydrates: 1g | Fat: 22g |
Sodium: 360mg | Fiber: 0g

Christmas Morning Eggs

Making this casserole the day before, doing all but the final baking, makes it settle well. On Christmas morning, you pop it in the oven and let it bake while opening gifts. In a snap, you've got an effortless holiday breakfast.

INGREDIENTS

7 slices low-carb wheat bread, torn into pieces

1 pound ground breakfast sausage or 1 pound bacon

12 eggs, beaten

16 ounces low-fat shredded Cheddar cheese, divided

¼ cup low-fat cream

Dash paprika, salt, and pepper

1. Preheat oven to 350°F.

2. Line bottom of 9" × 13" lightly greased baking dish with torn bread pieces.

3. Brown sausage or cook bacon and crumble into small pieces. Set aside.

4. Beat together eggs, ½ of cheese, and cream; pour over bread in baking dish. Top with sausage or bacon.

5. Sprinkle top with remaining cheese, paprika, salt, and pepper. If holding overnight, cover and refrigerate at this point.

6. Bake at 350°F for 20 minutes, or until golden brown and bubbly.

SERVES 6

Calories: 760 | Carbohydrates: 15g | Fat: 49g | Sodium: 2520mg | Fiber: 4g

Spicy Chilled Shrimp

*Keep the shrimp chilled and put the
serving bowl on ice while serving.*

INGREDIENTS

3 pounds uncooked shrimp, tail on,
    peeled and deveined

¾ cup olive oil

½ cup chopped fresh cilantro

¼ cup white wine vinegar

3 tablespoons fresh lemon juice

3 jalapeño chilies, seeded, minced

3 large cloves garlic, minced

¼ teaspoon cayenne pepper

Salt and freshly ground black
    pepper to taste

3 large lemons, sliced

1 large red onion, sliced

Is Spicy a Good Idea for Kids?

Absolutely. So much about
enjoying food is about the
taste sensations. If children
learn at a young age to appreciate interesting tastes, they
may also learn that quality and
variety trump quantity. Encourage new taste choices.

1. Bring a large pot of salted water to a
   boil. Add the shrimp; cook until pink
   and opaque, about 3 minutes. Using
   a slotted spoon, transfer the shrimp
   to a large bowl of ice water for 2
   minutes. Drain off water and place
   the shrimp in a large bowl in the
   refrigerator.

2. Whisk together the oil and the next
   6 ingredients in a medium-size bowl.
   Season with salt and pepper. Pour
   the marinade over the shrimp; toss
   to coat. Layer the shrimp, lemon
   slices, and onion in large glass bowl.
   Pour any remaining marinade over
   the shrimp. Cover and refrigerate for
   4 hours.

SERVES 12

Calories: 250 | Carbohydrates: 3g | Fat: 16g |
Sodium: 170mg | Fiber: 0g

Glazed Baked Ham with Rosemary

This ham tastes great served either hot or cold.
Serve it the next day as sandwiches.

INGREDIENTS

4-pound boneless ham

30 whole cloves

3 tablespoons Major Grey's
   Chutney

1 packed tablespoon dark brown
   sugar

2 tablespoons prepared
   horseradish mustard

2 teaspoons fresh rosemary leaves

Use It Again

Ham makes for great leftovers
that kids love. From ham salad
to a side meat at breakfast,
you'll find ways to use these
leftovers, so choose a large
ham.

1. Preheat the oven to 325°F.

2. Place the ham in a roasting pan set
   on a rack. Insert the whole cloves all
   over the ham. Bake for about 1½
   hours, or until the internal temperature reads 130°F.

3. Meanwhile, in a small saucepan
   combine the chutney, brown sugar,
   mustard, and rosemary. Cook over
   low heat until warm and liquefied.
   Drizzle the sauce all over the ham;
   bake for an additional 30 minutes, or
   until the internal temperature reads
   140°F. The outside of the ham
   should be crusty and sugary brown.

4. Allow the ham to rest for at least 15
   minutes before carving.

SERVES 12

Calories: 355 | Carbohydrates: 5.5g | Fat: 24g |
Sodium: 167.5mg | Fiber: 0g

Corn Bread Stuffing

Tastes best when eaten the same day it's made—
allow it to cool, covered, in the refrigerator until ready to serve.

INGREDIENTS

1 cup white or yellow cornmeal

1 cup all-purpose flour

2 tablespoons sugar

1 tablespoon baking powder

¼ teaspoon baking soda

¼ teaspoon salt

1¼ cups low-fat buttermilk or whole milk

¼ cup unsalted butter, melted

¼ cup vegetable oil

1 large egg

Measure but Don't Stress

Be sure to measure out carb-rich foods like this, but don't do it in a way that stresses your child. Use a cup measure and place a serving on each plate in the same shape, adding architecture to your presentation, rather than letting folks spoon it themselves. You'll maintain a carb count and have a pretty plate, too.

1. Preheat the oven to 350°F. Butter an 8" square baking pan.

2. In a large bowl, whisk together the cornmeal, flour, sugar, baking powder, baking soda, and salt.

3. In another bowl, whisk together the buttermilk or whole milk, melted butter, oil, and egg until smooth. Stir the wet into the dry ingredients, and when smooth and well mixed, pour the batter into the prepared pan. Bake for 35–40 minutes, or until a toothpick inserted near the center comes out clean, the cornbread begins to pull away from the sides of the pan, and the top is golden brown. Cool in the pan set on a wire rack. When cool, crumble into large pieces. Stuff into your turkey that has been baked halfway, or serve just as is.

SERVES 8

Calories: 260 | Carbohydrates: 31g | Fat: 14g | Sodium: 340mg | Fiber: 2g

Baked Stuffed Shrimp

Avocados taste very sweet, but they are actually low in carbs.
They are an excellent source of many vitamins and omega fats.

INGREDIENTS

3 tablespoons mayonnaise

2 medium-sized ripe avocados

Juice of 1 lime

Dash cayenne pepper

½ teaspoon salt

12 jumbo shrimp, peeled and
   butterflied

1. Preheat oven to 450°F. Using a fork, mash the first five ingredients together into a smooth paste.

2. Place a piece of aluminum foil on a baking sheet. Arrange the shrimp on the paper. Divide the avocado stuffing, placing an equal amount on each shrimp.

3. Bake for 8–10 minutes, or until the shrimp is pink and the stuffing hot.

YIELDS 4 SERVINGS; SERVING SIZE 4 OUNCES

Calories: 230 | Carbohydrates: 8g | Fat: 21g |
Sodium: 380mg | Fiber: 8g

Sparkly Carrots

*Use your favorite clear carbonated soda in this easy recipe.
It adds a slightly sweet crispness to this side dish.*

INGREDIENTS

1 tablespoon olive oil

2 shallots, minced

2 cups baby carrots

½ cup gluten-free lime
    carbonated soda

¼ teaspoon salt

⅛ teaspoon pepper

Fun Food Tricks!
(Wink, Wink)

It's okay to make eating right fun. Remember your mom telling you that eating carrots makes you see in the dark? Tell your child, and then after dinner go in a dark room and "see" what they can see that you "cannot!"

1. In large skillet, heat olive oil over medium heat. Add shallots; cook and stir until crisp-tender, about 2 minutes. Add carrots; cook and stir 2–3 minutes.

2. Add soda, salt, and pepper to skillet; bring to a boil. Reduce heat, cover, and simmer 4–5 minutes, or until carrots are tender. Serve immediately.

SERVES 4

Calories: 90 | Carbohydrates: 13g | Fat: 3.5g |
Sodium: 180mg | Fiber: 2g

Stuffed Bacon Mushrooms

If you use gluten-free bread crumbs,
this delicious appetizer becomes gluten free!

INGREDIENTS

16 large button mushrooms

Olive oil

4 slices bacon

1 onion, chopped

4 cloves garlic, minced

½ cup seasoned bread crumbs

⅔ cup soy-yogurt cheese

⅛ teaspoon cayenne pepper

¼ cup chopped flat-leaf parsley

1. Remove stems from mushrooms; trim ends off and then coarsely chop the stems. Place mushrooms gill-side up on a baking sheet and brush with olive oil. Preheat oven to 350°F.

2. Cook bacon in medium skillet over medium heat until crisp. Remove bacon to paper towels to drain. Crumble bacon; set aside. Remove all but 1 tablespoon bacon drippings from skillet.

3. Cook chopped mushroom stems, onion, and garlic in bacon drippings until tender, about 6–7 minutes. Remove from heat and stir in reserved bacon, bread crumbs, cheese, and cayenne pepper; mix well.

4. Stuff the mushroom caps with mixture. Bake 15–20 minutes, or until the stuffing is hot and bubbly. Sprinkle with parsley and serve immediately.

SERVES 8

Calories: 130 | Carbohydrates: 10g | Fat: 7g | Sodium: 390mg | Fiber: 1g

Spinach Fruit Salad

This sweet and tangy salad dressing is good on any mixed greens;
try it on coleslaw, too.

INGREDIENTS

½ cup sliced strawberries

1 tablespoon lemon juice

1 tablespoon sugar

¼ teaspoon salt

1 tablespoon gluten-free mustard

1 tablespoon minced onion

¼ cup apple juice

¼ cup extra-virgin olive oil

6 cups baby spinach

2 cups watercress

2 cups sliced strawberries

1 cup raspberries

1. In food processor or blender, combine strawberries, lemon juice, sugar, salt, mustard, minced onion, apple juice, and olive oil; process or blend until smooth. Cover and refrigerate up to 3 days.

2. In serving bowl, toss together spinach, watercress, 2 cups strawberries, and raspberries. Drizzle with ½ of the dressing; toss again. Serve immediately with remaining dressing on the side.

SERVES 6

Calories: 90 | Carbohydrates: 12g | Fat: 5g | Sodium: 105mg | Fiber: 4g

Chili Cheese Corn Casserole

An easy dish to prepare the day before
an outdoor picnic or Big Game party.

INGREDIENTS

4 cups fresh corn kernels (or
  frozen, thawed and drained)

1 cup grated Cheddar cheese

1 (8-ounce) package cream cheese,
  at room temperature

1 (7-ounce) can diced green chilies

2 teaspoons chili powder

2 teaspoons ground cumin

1. Preheat oven to 350°F. Butter a 1½-quart baking dish.

2. Mix all the ingredients in a large bowl until well blended. Transfer to the prepared baking dish; bake until bubbling, about 30 minutes. Let cool, then cover and refrigerate up to 1 day. To serve, gently reheat, covered, in a 350°F oven for about 30 minutes, until heated throughout.

SERVES 8

Calories: 250 | Carbohydrates: 23g | Fat: 15g | Sodium: 190mg | Fiber: 3g

Balsamic-Marinated Beef Tenderloin

This delicious recipe is also great on the grill.
Any extra balsamic glaze also works well on roasted vegetables.

INGREDIENTS

6 (5-ounce) 1" thick beef
tenderloin fillets

½ cup extra-virgin olive oil, plus
extra for grilling

½ cup plus 2 tablespoons
balsamic vinegar

2 tablespoons very finely chopped
fresh rosemary

Salt and coarsely ground black
pepper

1. Place the meat in a shallow casse-role dish.

2. In a small bowl, mix together the olive oil, 2 tablespoons of balsamic vinegar, and the rosemary; pour over the fillets, turning the meat to ensure the steaks are evenly coated.

3. Let marinate in the refrigerator, covered, for 2 hours, turning the fillets after 1 hour.

4. Remove the fillets from the marinade. Sprinkle salt and pepper on both sides.

5. Coat a grill pan or sauté pan lightly with oil. Preheat the pan until very hot, almost smoking, and cook the fillets for about 3–4 minutes on each side for medium-rare. (Increase cooking time by 2-minute increments per side for each further degree of doneness: medium, medium-well, and well-done.)

Balsamic-Marinated Beef Tenderloin

(continued)

Tenderloin for All!

Spending a little more on a cut of meat is well worth it, not just for the holidays, but simply for the pleasure of seeing your child eat his meal with gusto and enjoyment.

6. Place the remaining ½ cup balsamic vinegar in small saucepan; cook over medium heat until reduced to about half (¼ cup).

7. Let the fillets sit for a few minutes after they are done cooking; drizzle with a little of the reduced balsamic vinegar. Serve immediately.

SERVES 6

Calories: 610 | Carbohydrates: 9g | Fat: 51g | Sodium: 75mg | Fiber: 0g

Grilled Beef and Onion Kebabs

An easy summer recipe that will please everyone!

INGREDIENTS

4 teaspoons finely ground coriander seeds

4 teaspoons finely ground anise seeds

1 tablespoon minced garlic

1 tablespoon ground paprika

¼ teaspoon cayenne pepper

½ cup olive oil, divided

Salt and freshly ground black pepper to taste

1½ pounds boneless sirloin steak, fat trimmed, cut into 1¼" cubes

12 red pearl onions (about 3 ounces), peeled and cut in half lengthwise

Summer Skewer Fun

Try some unusual twists on skewers: *Fruit skewers*—Use colorful bites of strawberries, grapes, and melon pieces. *Greek island skewers*—Petite pieces of feta cheese skewered with broiled cherry tomatoes (count 1 gram of carbohydrate per cherry tomato) and pitted kalamata olives. This is an attractive presentation with fresh rosemary branches used for the skewers.

1. Preheat a grill or grill pan until hot.

2. Place the ground coriander and anise seeds in a medium-size bowl. Add the garlic, paprika, cayenne pepper, and ¼ cup of the olive oil. Season the marinade with salt and pepper; stir until combined. Add the sirloin cubes and stir to coat; set aside.

3. In a medium-size bowl, combine the onions and the remaining ¼ cup olive oil. Season with salt and pepper; toss to coat.

4. Divide the steaks among 4 skewers; thread, leaving ½" between each cube. Divide the onions among another 4 skewers; thread.

5. Grill the sirloin kebobs until well browned and medium-rare; grill the onion until glistening, tender, and slightly charred, 5–7 minutes for both. Serve on the skewers.

SERVES 4

Calories: 520 | Carbohydrates: 6g | Fat: 40g | Sodium: 95mg | Fiber: 2g

Country Ham

A country ham is a beautiful thing!
Depending on where they come from, country hams
are smoked or salt cured. Both are improved by soaking.

INGREDIENTS

10-pound country ham, bone in

Water to cover

10 bay leaves

1 pound brown sugar

20 whole cloves, bruised

25 peppercorns, bruised

10 coriander seeds, bruised

½ cup brown sugar

2 tablespoons dark mustard

½ teaspoon powdered cloves

1½ cups apple cider

Bruising

To bruise garlic or any food, you should place the flat side of a knife against the clove and quickly whack the knife once with your hand to soften but not break the clove.

1. Prepare the ham by removing skin and most of the fat, leaving ¼" of fat.

2. Soak ham in water to cover with bay leaves, 1 pound brown sugar, cloves, peppercorns, and coriander seeds for 30 hours in your fridge.

3. Preheat the oven to 300°F. Pat the ham dry and place in a roasting pan. Mix together ½ cup brown sugar, the mustard, and the cloves.

4. Bake for 3½ hours, basting with the apple cider. You can degrease the pan juices and use the apple cider as a sauce; otherwise, serve with applesauce.

SERVES 20

Per serving:
Calories: 560 | Carbohydrates: 31g | Fat: 19g | Sodium: 6150mg | Fiber: <1g

Pumpkin Pie with Macadamia Nut Crust

A delicious do-ahead dessert—
this recipe requires a few mixing bowls, but is worth the effort.

INGREDIENTS

1½ cups finely chopped
    macadamia nuts

16 packets sugar substitute

2 tablespoons butter, softened,
    plus extra for greasing

1 (1-ounce) packet gelatin

¼ cup water

1 teaspoon pumpkin pie spice

1 (15-ounce) can canned pumpkin

2 teaspoons grated orange zest

1½ cups heavy cream

2 teaspoons vanilla extract

1. Heat oven to 400°F. Butter the bottom and sides of a 9" springform pan.

2. In a medium-size bowl, combine the macadamia nuts, 4 packets of sugar substitute, and 2 tablespoons butter; mix well.

3. Press the mixture onto the bottom and 1" up the sides of the prepared pan. Bake for 10 minutes, until golden brown. Cool on a wire rack.

4. In a small bowl, sprinkle the gelatin over the water; let sit for 5 minutes, until the gelatin softens.

5. Heat a small skillet over medium heat; toast the pumpkin pie spice for 1–2 minutes, until fragrant, stirring frequently. Reduce heat to low; stir in the gelatin mixture and cook 1–2 minutes, until the gelatin melts. Remove from heat and cool to room temperature.

6. Place the pumpkin purée in a large bowl; mash with a fork to loosen. Mix in the orange zest.

Pumpkin Pie with Macadamia Nut Crust

(continued)

Canned Pumpkin

When a recipe calls for canned pumpkin, be sure that you buy and use what is called "solid pack" pumpkin. If you buy canned pumpkin pie pudding, the recipe will fail because that ingredient contains sugar, emulsifiers, and liquids in addition to pumpkin. If you're feeling ambitious, you could cook and purée a fresh pumpkin and use that instead.

7. In another large bowl, using an electric mixer on high speed, beat the cream with the remaining 12 packets of sugar substitute and the vanilla until soft peaks form.

8. With a rubber spatula, slowly fold in the gelatin mixture (if it's too stiff, heat on the stove until melted but not hot). In 3 parts, gently fold the whipped cream mixture into the pumpkin purée.

9. Pour the filling into the cooled macadamia nut pie crust; smooth the top. Refrigerate at least 3 hours before serving.

SERVES 8

Calories: 400 | Carbohydrates: 11g | Fat: 39g | Sodium: 30mg | Fiber: 4g

Pumpkin Soup (Savory)

Pumpkin soup is fine any time of year. You can use canned pumpkin, which is very good, but be sure to buy unsweetened and unflavored pumpkin so that you don't end up with soup that tastes like pumpkin pie!

INGREDIENTS

1 teaspoon butter

1 cup yellow onion, chopped

1½ cups chicken broth

¼ cup dry white wine

1 teaspoon sage leaves, dried, or
    4 fresh sage leaves, chopped

½ teaspoon oregano, dried

2 cups canned pumpkin

Salt to taste

1 teaspoon Tabasco sauce

Garnish of chopped fresh chives

½ cup heavy cream

⅛ pound smoked ham, chopped,
    for garnish

You could also substitute olive oil for butter and whole milk for heavy cream

1. Melt the butter in a soup kettle. Add onion; sauté over medium-low heat for 5 minutes. Stir in all remaining ingredients but the heavy cream and ham.

2. Simmer the soup, covered, for 10 minutes. Add heavy cream. Serve hot with ham sprinkled on top.

SERVES 4

Calories: 200 | Carbohydrates: 16g | Fat: 13g | Sodium: 480mg | Fiber: 4g

Pumpkin Soup (Slightly Sweet)

If you have a sweet tooth,
you can add some more brown sugar to this recipe.

INGREDIENTS

1 cup Vidalia or other sweet onion, finely chopped

½" fresh gingerroot, peeled and minced

2 cups orange juice

2 cups chicken broth

1 (15-ounce) can canned pumpkin

1 teaspoon brown sugar

½ teaspoon ground cinnamon

¼ teaspoon ground nutmeg

¼ teaspoon ground cloves

Salt and pepper to taste

* Optional: ½ cup heavy cream

1. Stir the ingredients into the soup pot, one by one, whisking after each addition.

2. Cover and simmer for 10 minutes. If you decide to use the cream, add at the last minute.

SERVES 4

Calories: 120 | Carbohydrates: 27g | Fat: 1g | Sodium: 400mg | Fiber: 4g

CHAPTER 8

Birthday Parties and Sleepovers

Vanilla Ice Cream

*You don't have to have
an ice cream machine to make this!*

INGREDIENTS

1 quart heavy cream

6 egg yolks

1 quart whole milk

1 cup Equal Spoonful

½ teaspoon salt

2 tablespoons vanilla extract

3 egg whites

1. Oil a 9" × 5" metal bread loaf pan. Line the pan with 2 layers of plastic wrap, leaving at least a 4" overhang on the long sides. Freeze the pan for 30 minutes.

2. Using an electric mixer, whip the heavy cream until it thickens but is still somewhat loose (before soft peaks form). Beat in the egg yolks, whole milk, sweetener, salt, and vanilla until the mixture is not quite as thick as regular whipped cream.

3. In a separate bowl, beat the egg whites until they hold soft peaks. Fold the egg whites into the whipped mixture until uniformly blended. Pour the mixture into the chilled pan, cover with foil, and freeze 12–24 hours, until solid. (If you have an ice cream machine, add the mixture to the prepared machine following the manufacturer's instructions.)

4. Place your food processor bowl and blade in the freezer. Dip the metal loaf pan into hot water for 5 seconds to ease in removing the

Vanilla Ice Cream

(continued)

Homemade Tastes Better

There is something about making it yourself that makes everything taste great. Enlist the help of your child in making this ice cream before the party and she will say it's the best she's ever had.

plastic-wrapped ice cream. Firmly pull up on the plastic wrap and remove the ice cream loaf. Peel off the plastic wrap.

5. Cut the loaf into thick slices with a large knife, slicing off only the amount desired to be served. Cut each slice into 4 chunks; immediately put into the chilled food processor bowl and begin to process in 5-second pulses, adding as little milk or cream as needed to make the ice cream smooth. Scrape down the sides of the bowl as necessary. Serve immediately when the ice cream is smooth in texture, or freeze to hold for several minutes if serving as an accompaniment to another dessert.

SERVES 12

Calories: 390 | Carbohydrates: 23g | Fat: 34g | Sodium: 180mg | Fiber: 0g

Sugar-Free Chocolate Sauce

This sauce will keep for weeks in the refrigerator. Use it as a base for other desserts or spoon it over ice cream and frozen sugar-free yogurt.

INGREDIENTS

⅓ cup Dutch process cocoa powder

2 tablespoons Splenda or to taste

¼ teaspoon salt

1 tablespoon cornstarch

1 teaspoon instant espresso

1 cup cold water

1. Whisk all ingredients together until all of the lumps are gone.

2. Place in a saucepan over medium heat. Bring to a boil, whisking until thickened. Taste and add more Splenda if necessary.

3. Let cool; pour into a jar for use as needed. Store in the refrigerator.

YIELDS 1 CUP; SERVING SIZE 2 TABLESPOONS

Calories: 20 | Carbohydrates: 3g | Fat: 3.5g | Sodium: 75mg | Fiber: <1g

Tortilla Chips

By choosing nonfat corn tortillas and being careful about the amount of oil you use to coat them, you can create snack chips that are lower in fat than most baked commercial varieties. You also control the sodium content!

INGREDIENTS

1 nonfat corn tortilla

1 tablespoon olive oil

Sea salt to taste (optional)

Seasoning blend of your choice, to taste

Plan-Ahead Bowls

True, your child has to account for every carb he eats, but you can still make a party feel carefree by counting out bowls of chips ahead of time and encouraging each kid to grab a bowl and go nuts. Your child will feel just like all the other snackers.

1. Preheat oven to 400°F.

2. Spray or rub both sides of the tortilla with olive oil. Season lightly with sea salt or any seasoning blend.

3. Bake the tortillas on a cookie sheet until crisp and beginning to brown, about 2–5 minutes, depending on the thickness of the tortilla.

4. Break the tortillas into large pieces.

SERVES 1

Calories: 180 | Carbohydrates: 12g | Fat: 14g | Sodium: 10mg | Fiber: 2g

Stuffed Celery

*This unique take on stuffed celery is wonderful,
replacing peanut butter or cream cheese with luxurious, buttery Brie.*

INGREDIENTS

Wide ends of 6 celery stalks, cut
in halves

5 ounces Brie cheese, softened

2 tablespoons capers

3 tablespoons chopped walnuts,
toasted

1. Lay the celery pieces on a cool serving plate. Remove the skin from the Brie and mash it with a fork. Mix in the capers.

2. Stuff each piece of celery and garnish with toasted walnuts or with raisins à la "ants on a log."

MAKES 12 PIECES STUFFED CELERY

Calories: 60 | Carbohydrates: 2g | Fat: 4.5g |
Sodium: 140mg | Fiber: <1g

Turkey Chili

*This recipe has a few nice Texas-style bells and whistles.
You can cook this classic for just a few hours or overnight—
the longer the better. Kids love the turkey taste.*

INGREDIENTS

¼ cup vegetable oil

2½ pounds lean ground turkey meat

4 sweet red onions, chopped

6 cloves garlic, chopped

4 Italian green frying peppers, stemmed, seeded, and chopped

2 large sweet red bell peppers, roasted

2 sweet yellow peppers, stemmed, seeded, and chopped

4 jalapeño peppers, stemmed, seeded, and chopped

2 tablespoons chili powder, or to taste

1 tablespoon dry English-style mustard

1 teaspoon cinnamon

1 teaspoon Dutch process cocoa powder

½ cup strong cold coffee

2 tablespoons Splenda

3 (14-ounce) cans red kidney beans, drained and rinsed

2 (28-ounce) cans sugar-free Italian plum tomatoes

Salt and pepper to taste

1 teaspoon liquid smoke, or to taste

1. Heat the oil over medium heat in a large pot that has a cover. Sauté the turkey, breaking it up with a wooden spoon. Add the onions, garlic, and peppers to the pot. Stir, sautéing until softened, about 12 minutes.

2. Add the chili powder to the meat mixture; stir to combine. In a separate bowl, blend the dry mustard, cinnamon, and cocoa powder with the coffee. Whisk with a fork until smooth. Add to the meat mixture.

3. Stir in remaining ingredients and cover. Reduce the heat to a bare simmer. Cook for a minimum of 3 hours.

YIELDS 12 SERVINGS; SERVING SIZE 6 OUNCES

Calories: 330 | Carbohydrates: 29g | Fat: 14g | Sodium: 570mg | Fiber: 8g

Tiny Italian Meatballs with Pine Nuts

*These doll-sized meatballs can also be fried,
which does add to the calorie count. However, baking works well;
just don't overcook them or they'll dry out.*

INGREDIENTS

1 pound lean ground sirloin

3 cloves garlic, minced

½ cup dried sugar-free
    breadcrumbs

1 whole egg, beaten

1 teaspoon Splenda

½ teaspoon ground cinnamon

1 teaspoon salt

1 teaspoon dried oregano leaves

⅔ cup pine nuts

½ cup raisins with no sugar added
    (optional)

1. Preheat oven to 375°F. Prepare 2 cookie sheets with nonstick spray. Mix all ingredients thoroughly with your fingers.

2. Roll into marble-sized meatballs, about ¾" in diameter. Bake for 8–10 minutes, turning the cookie sheets once to make sure they all get equal heat.

3. Serve on toothpicks, in sauce, or in mini hero sandwiches.

**YIELDS 70 MEATBALLS;
SERVING SIZE 3 MEATBALLS**

Calories: 70 | Carbohydrates: 5g | Fat: 4g |
Sodium: 130mg | Fiber: <1g

Stick 'Em Up!

There is something about kids and toothpicks. They'll eat just about anything in this way. Consider a meats-on-a-stick theme for the party, letting the kids spear their yummy treats.

Barbecue Wings

Wings are usually fried and dipped in a mix of butter, vinegar, and hot sauce. This is more traditional, less fattening, and just as delicious. You have the option to either steam or boil the wings prior to adding barbecue sauce.

INGREDIENTS

30 whole chicken wings

1 quart water

1 cup barbecue sauce

Tabasco sauce to taste

1. Remove the wing tips and halve the wings. Meanwhile, bring water to a boil.

2. Drop the wings into boiling water. Cover, reduce heat, and boil gently for 10 minutes. Preheat the broiler or indoor grill to 400°F.

3. Drain off the broth, reserving for stock. Prepare a broiler pan or indoor grill with nonstick spray.

4. Mix the barbecue sauce and Tabasco sauce together to your liking. Brush the wings with the combined sauce and grill until browned. Can be served hot with extra sugar-free barbecue sauce on the side.

**YIELD 10 SERVINGS;
SERVING SIZE 3 WHOLE WINGS**

Calories: 370 | Carbohydrates: 8g | Fat: 25g | Sodium: 400mg | Fiber: 0g

Melting Tea Cakes

These tender cookies crumble when you bite into them,
then they melt in your mouth. If you'd like a spicier cookie, add cinnamon.

INGREDIENTS

1 cup butter, softened

½ cup gluten-free powdered
sugar

2 teaspoons gluten-free vanilla

1½ cups superfine rice flour

½ cup white sorghum flour

¼ cup cornstarch or tapioca flour

¼ teaspoon salt

¼ teaspoon ground cardamom

1 teaspoon xanthan gum

More gluten-free powdered
sugar for rolling (up to 2
tablespoons)

Party Time

Dress up these tea-party cookies by displaying them on doilies, and let the kids dip them into warm cups of decaf tea.

1. Preheat oven to 400°F. In large bowl, beat butter until fluffy. Add powdered sugar and vanilla; beat until blended. Stir in remaining ingredients except additional powdered sugar.

2. Form dough into balls about ¾" in diameter. Place on ungreased cookie sheet. Bake 8–13 minutes, or until cookies are very light golden brown on the bottom.

3. Immediately drop hot cookies into powdered sugar and roll to coat. Place on wire rack until cool, then reroll in powdered sugar. Store covered at room temperature.

YIELDS 36 COOKIES

Calories: 80 | Carbohydrates: 9g | Fat: 5g | Sodium: 15mg | Fiber: 0g

Orange Cups with Lemon Cream

*This dish must be served the same day it's prepared
or the filling will start to separate.*

INGREDIENTS

4 large oranges

Grated zest of 1 lemon

⅓ cup light whipping cream

½ cup vanilla yogurt

Julienne strips of lemon and
   orange peel for garnish

Finding Low-Carb Online

There are a number of new websites offering low-carb sweets. Try the following sites to purchase premade sugar-free desserts and products: *www.locarbdiner.com.*

1. With a sharp knife, cut each orange in half crosswise. Remove the flesh (with the help of a grapefruit spoon) and chop finely; place in a bowl. Set the hollowed out orange halves aside.

2. Mix the lemon zest with the chopped orange flesh. In a separate bowl, whip the cream until it is stiff. With a rubber spatula, fold the yogurt into the whipped cream. Add the cream mixture to the chopped oranges; stir gently to mix. Very thinly slice the bottom off each reserved orange shell so they sit level on a plate.

3. Fill all the shells with the orange mixture; place on a serving plate. Refrigerate the filled shells until ready to serve. To serve, decorate with lemon and orange peel strips.

SERVES 8

Calories: 100 | Carbohydrates: 16g | Fat: 4.5g |
Sodium: 15mg | Fiber: 5g

Peppermint Patties GF

*There's even mint in the chocolate coating in this easy candy recipe.
Your kids will love it.*

INGREDIENTS

4 cups gluten-free powdered
    sugar

⅛ teaspoon salt

3 tablespoons dairy-free vegan
    margarine, softened

1 tablespoon gluten-free corn
    syrup

2 teaspoons gluten-free
    peppermint extract

½ teaspoon gluten-free mint
    extract

¼ cup rice milk

2 cups gluten-free semisweet,
    mint-flavored chocolate chips

1. In large bowl, combine sugar and salt; mix well. Add margarine, corn syrup, both extracts, and rice milk; beat with electric mixer until thoroughly combined. You may need to add more sugar or rice milk to reach desired consistency.

2. Roll mixture into 1" balls; place on waxed paper-lined cookie sheet. Flatten with bottom of drinking glass to ¼" thickness. Cover; chill 1 hour.

3. Place 1½ cups of chocolate chips in microwave-safe glass measuring cup. Melt chocolate on half power 2 minutes; remove and stir. Microwave on half power at 30-second intervals, stirring after each interval, until chocolate is melted and smooth. Add remaining ½ cup of chips; stir constantly until they are also melted.

4. Dip the peppermint centers into the chocolate mixture, shaking off excess. Place on cookie sheet and chill until chocolate is set.

YIELDS 48 CANDIES

Calories: 100 | Carbohydrates: 16g | Fat: 3.5g |
Sodium: 15mg | Fiber: <1g

Miniature Crab Cakes

Traditionally, crab cakes are fried in butter. This healthy alternative bakes them. It also takes advantage of panko, a type of breadcrumb that adds a lot of crunch to a dish without adding a lot of fat.

INGREDIENTS

8 ounces crabmeat

¼ cup mayonnaise

Juice and zest of ½ lemon

1 egg

1 tablespoon chili sauce

2 tablespoons sweet white onion, minced

1 teaspoon dried dill weed or 1 tablespoon fresh dill, snipped

1 teaspoon dry Dijon-style mustard blended with 2 teaspoons water

½ cup panko

1. Preheat the oven to 450°F. Prepare a baking sheet with nonstick spray.

2. Mix all ingredients except the panko together in a bowl. Spread the panko breadcrumbs on a piece of waxed paper.

3. Make little "burgers" using about 1 tablespoonful of the crab mixture for each. Coat with panko.

4. Bake for 5 minutes. Turn and bake for another 5 minutes, or until very crisp. Serve on slices of cucumber, leaves of romaine lettuce, or small pieces of bread.

So Young and Yet So Sophisticated

Young partygoers will feel grown up and exotic with this healthy but special choice of nibblers. Teach manners while serving (using a cocktail napkin, etc.).

YIELDS 16 CAKES; SERVING SIZE 2 CRAB CAKES

Calories: 120 | Carbohydrates: 6g | Fat: 7g | Sodium: 230mg | Fiber: 0g

Artichoke and Spinach Dip

Serve this dip in a hollowed round loaf of bread. Surround the dip with crackers or thinly sliced pieces of sugar-free sourdough baguette.

INGREDIENTS

10 ounces frozen chopped spinach, thawed

1 cup artichoke hearts, drained

8 ounces low-fat cream cheese at room temperature

½ cup sweet onion, minced

Juice of ½ lemon

¼ cup mayonnaise

¼ cup low-fat sour cream

½ teaspoon cayenne pepper

⅛ teaspoon nutmeg

1 teaspoon Splenda

1 tablespoon Parmesan cheese

1. Preheat oven to 350°F. Squeeze the moisture out of the spinach; press the oil out of the artichokes. Purée all ingredients except the Parmesan cheese in a food processor.

2. Prepare a 1-quart baking dish with nonstick spray. Transfer the spinach dip into the dish. Sprinkle with Parmesan cheese. Bake for 30 minutes.

SERVES 20;
SERVING SIZE 3 TEASPOONS ON 3 CRACKERS

For dip only:
Calories: 60 | Carbohydrates: 3g | Fat: 4.5g | Sodium: 90mg | Fiber: 0g

No-Gluten Peanut Butter Cookies

Yes, this recipe really works! Just be sure to bake the cookies on parchment paper, foil, or Silpat silicone liners, because they stick to even greased cookie sheets.

INGREDIENTS

2 cups crunchy natural peanut butter

½ cup sugar

½ cup gluten-free powdered sugar

1 cup dark brown sugar

2 eggs

1 teaspoon baking soda

2 tablespoons granulated sugar for rolling

Powdered Sugar Done Homestyle

Most powdered sugar has cornstarch added to prevent lumps and help stabilize whipped cream and other soft mixtures. You can make your own powdered sugar. Combine regular granulated sugar with a pinch of arrowroot powder in a blender and blend until very fine. Use as a substitute for powdered sugar in any recipe.

1. In large bowl, combine all ingredients except the extra granulated sugar. Cover; chill in refrigerator until dough is firm.

2. Preheat oven to 350°F. Roll dough into 1" balls; roll in sugar. Place on parchment paper, foil, or Silpat-lined cookie sheets. Using a fork, flatten balls with a crosshatch pattern. Bake 8–9 minutes, or until cookies are set. Let cool on cookie sheet 5 minutes, then carefully remove to wire rack to cool completely.

YIELDS 24 COOKIES

Calories: 190 | Carbohydrates: 20g | Fat: 11g | Sodium: 150mg | Fiber: 1g

Gluten-Free Caramels

How much fun is it for kids to make their own party candies?
Make this a group project to take up party activity time.

INGREDIENTS

Unsalted butter for greasing

1 cup sugar

1 cup brown sugar

1 cup gluten-free light corn syrup

½ teaspoon salt

½ cup gluten-free dark corn syrup

2 cups heavy cream

¾ cup unsalted butter, room temperature

2 teaspoons gluten-free vanilla

1. Grease a 13" × 9" baking pan with unsalted butter and set aside.

2. In large heavy saucepan, combine sugar, brown sugar, light corn syrup, salt, and dark corn syrup; bring to a boil over medium heat, stirring frequently.

3. Reduce heat to low; gradually stir in cream, whisking constantly.

4. Add butter; stir until melted.

5. Attach a candy thermometer to side of pan, making sure it doesn't touch the bottom.

6. Cook candy over low heat until temperature reaches 240°F. (*To cook without a candy thermometer:* When mixture thickens and boiling begins to slow down, start testing by dropping a bit of the hot candy into cold water. When it forms a firm ball that can still be shaped with your fingers, remove it from the heat.)

Gluten-Free Caramels GF

(continued)

Thermometer Know-How

There are quite a few different types of candy thermometers; all work well as long as you follow a few rules. Make sure that the thermometer bulb is totally immersed in the boiling candy, but is not touching the bottom or sides of the pan. Rinse the thermometer with hot water to bring it up to temperature more quickly, and cool it slowly at room temperature.

7. Remove pan from heat; stir in vanilla (be careful, mixture will boil up and steam).

8. Pour into prepared pan. Let stand until cool.

9. Cut into squares and wrap individually in parchment paper.

YIELDS 48 CANDIES

Calories: 120 | Carbohydrates: 17g | Fat: 7g | Sodium: 45mg | Fiber: 0g

No-Bake Honey Balls

*These sweet and chewy no-bake cookies
are a good choice for beginning cooks.*

INGREDIENTS

½ cup honey

½ cup gluten-free golden raisins

½ cup gluten-free dry milk powder

1 cup crushed crisp rice cereal

¼ cup gluten-free powdered
   sugar

1 cup finely chopped dates

1 cup crushed crisp rice cereal

Care with Dates

Do not buy the precut dates
that have been coated in sugar
for most recipes. They are too
dry and too sweet and will
upset the balance of most recipes. To chop dates, use scis-
sors occasionally dipped into
very hot water. If you can find
them, Medjool dates, usually
found in health food and gour-
met stores, are richer than the
Deglet Noor dates commonly
found in your local mega-mart.

1. In food processor, combine honey
   and raisins; process until smooth.
   Scrape into a small bowl and add
   milk powder, 1 cup crushed cereal,
   powdered sugar, and dates; mix well.
   You may need to add more powdered sugar or honey for desired
   consistency.

2. Form mixture into ¾" balls; roll in
   remaining 1 cup crushed cereal.
   Store tightly covered at room
   temperature.

YIELDS 30 COOKIES

Calories: 60 | Carbohydrates: 15g | Fat: 0.5g |
Sodium: 20mg | Fiber: <1g

CHAPTER 9

Picnics and Cookouts

Turkey Mushroom Burgers

*If you want to cook all of the burgers at once, allow any extras to
cool and then wrap them each in individual foil packets.
Place those packets in a labeled freezer bag and freeze until needed.*

INGREDIENTS

1 pound turkey breast

1 pound fresh button mushrooms

1 tablespoon olive oil

1 teaspoon butter

1 clove garlic, minced

1 tablespoon chopped green
onion

¼ teaspoon dried thyme

¼ teaspoon dried oregano

¼ teaspoon freshly ground black
pepper

Cayenne pepper or dried red
pepper flakes to taste
(optional)

1. Cut the turkey into even pieces about 1" square. Place the turkey cubes in the freezer for 10 minutes, or long enough to allow the turkey to become somewhat firm.

2. In a covered microwave-safe container, microwave the mushrooms on high 3–4 minutes, or until they begin to soften and sweat. Set aside to cool slightly.

3. Process the turkey in a food processor until ground, scraping down the sides of the bowl as necessary. Add the oil, butter, garlic, onion, and mushrooms (and any resulting liquid from the mushrooms); process until the mushrooms are ground, again scraping down the sides of the bowl as necessary. Add the remaining ingredients; pulse until mixed. Shape into 8 equal-sized patties. Cooking times will vary according to the method used and how thick you form the burgers.

YIELDS 8 LARGE BURGERS

Calories: 100 | Carbohydrates: 2g | Fat: 2.5g |
Sodium: 30mg | Fiber: <1g

Layered Salad

Layered salads are great because of their staying power: the longer it waits, the better it is, so it travels well. This version is still a little high in fat, so if you can tolerate fat-free mayonnaise and fat-free sour cream, try using those.

INGREDIENTS

¼ cup mayonnaise

1¼ cups nonfat cottage cheese

½ cup nonfat plain yogurt

1 tablespoon apple cider vinegar or lemon juice

Pinch of sugar

6 cups shredded mixed lettuce

1½ cups diced celery

1½ cups chopped onion, any variety

1½ cups sliced carrots

1½ cups frozen green peas, thawed

6 ounces (2% fat or less) smoked turkey breast

6 ounces Cheddar cheese, shredded (to yield 1½ cups)

1. Combine the mayonnaise, cottage cheese, yogurt, vinegar or lemon juice, and sugar in a food processor or blender; process until smooth. Set aside.

2. In a large salad bowl, layer the lettuce, celery, onion, carrots, peas, and turkey breast. Spread the mayonnaise mixture over the top of the salad. Top with the shredded cheese.

Mock Mayo

Spread a little flavor! Measure ½ teaspoon drained nonfat yogurt into a paper coffee filter. Twist to secure; drain over a cup or bowl in the refrigerator for at least 1 hour. In a small bowl, combine the drained yogurt with ½ teaspoon mayonnaise. Use as you would mayonnaise. Serving size is 1 teaspoon. Calories: 11.52; Carbohydrates: 0.86g; Fat: 0.82g; Cholesterol: 0.70mg; Sodium: 20.11mg; Fiber: 0.00g.

SERVES 6

Calories: 310 | Carbohydrates: 19g | Fat: 17g | Sodium: 670mg | Fiber: 5g

Grilled Shrimp on Skewers

When you marinate shrimp, be careful not to leave it in an acidic marinade for more than the recommended time. The lime juice adds flavor, but it will also "cook" your shrimp if left too long.

INGREDIENTS

4 wooden skewers, soaked in water for 1 hour

6 jumbo shrimp, cleaned and deveined

Juice of 1 lime

¼ cup soy sauce

2 cloves garlic, minced

1" gingerroot, peeled and minced

2 tablespoons Asian fish sauce

¼ cup peanut oil

1 red pepper, cored, seeded, and cut in wedges

1 medium zucchini, ends removed, cut in 1" pieces

6 large brown mushrooms

1. Marinate shrimp for 1 hour in a mixture of lime juice, soy sauce, garlic, gingerroot, fish sauce, and peanut oil.

2. Thread all the shrimp on one skewer; use the other three for the red pepper, zucchini, and mushrooms.

3. Broil or grill the vegetables for 6 minutes, turning often. Add the shrimp skewer; grill for about 2 minutes per side, or until shrimp turns pink.

SERVES 2

Calories: 370 | Carbohydrates: 16g | Fat: 28g | Sodium: 3480mg | Fiber: 3g

Skewer with Care

Wooden skewers must be pre-soaked to prevent them from burning. Metal skewers work fine, but they have to be washed after using, whereas you just dispose of the wooden ones.

Fried Chicken with Cornmeal Crust

Coarsely grated cornmeal makes an excellent crust for fried chicken. There are people who use corn muffin mix as the coating for their chicken. While that's fine, it's more wholesome to make your own crust.

INGREDIENTS

4 half-breasts chicken (4 ounces each), boneless and skinless

½ cup low-fat buttermilk

½ cup coarse cornmeal

1 teaspoon baking powder

½ teaspoon salt

Freshly ground pepper to taste

½" canola or other oil in a deep pan for frying

1. Soak the chicken in buttermilk for 15 minutes. On a piece of waxed paper, mix the cornmeal, baking powder, salt, and pepper. Coat the chicken with the cornmeal mixture.

2. In a large frying pan, heat the oil to 350°F. Fry 8–10 minutes per side. Drain on paper towels. Excellent served cold.

SERVES 4

Calories: 190 | Carbohydrates: 14g | Fat: 2g | Sodium: 520mg | Fiber: 1g

Picnic Stuffed Hard-Boiled Eggs

These stuffed eggs travel beautifully and make any picnic special.
Enjoy them anywhere—at the beach, on a mountaintop, or in the car.

INGREDIENTS

¼ pound crabmeat

¼ cup mayonnaise

Juice of ½ lemon

½ teaspoon Old Bay seasoning or chili powder

6 hard-boiled eggs, halved, yolks removed from whites

1 teaspoon Worcestershire sauce

½ teaspoon dried dill weed

Freshly ground black pepper to taste

Is There a Best Way to Hard-Boil Eggs?

Start with very fresh eggs. Using a pin, make a very small hole in the larger end of each egg. Place the eggs in cold water. Start them over high flame. When they come to a boil, reduce heat to very low. Let cook for 5 minutes. Turn off heat. Let eggs sit for another 4–5 minutes. Run pan of eggs under cold water. Crack and peel as soon as possible.

1. Mix the crabmeat, mayonnaise, lemon juice, and Old Bay seasoning or chili powder.

2. Set cooked egg-white halves on a serving platter. Mash the egg yolks together. Using a fork, mix them with the crabmeat mixture and Worcestershire sauce. Sprinkle with dill weed and pepper. Pile on the egg whites.

3. Wrap stuffed eggs individually with foil if packing for picnic. Or serve on a platter, with cucumber slices separating stuffed eggs to keep them from rolling around.

YIELDS 6 SERVINGS; SERVING SIZE 1 EGG

Calories: 160 | Carbohydrates: 1g | Fat: 13g | Sodium: 190mg | Fiber: 0g

Spicy Chicken Burgers

Adjust the cayenne pepper and chili powder in this easy recipe to your family's tastes. (Some kids like milder.) Serve on toasted buns or plain.

INGREDIENTS

1 tablespoon olive oil

½ onion, chopped

½ cup minced leek

½ cup grated carrot

1 slice French bread, crumbled

2 tablespoons mustard (of your choice)

½ teaspoon salt

⅛ teaspoon cayenne pepper

2 teaspoons chili powder

½ teaspoon cumin

1¼ pounds ground gluten-free chicken

Doing the Chicken Grind

It may be difficult to find ground chicken in your supermarket. You can buy chicken breasts and thighs and ask the butcher to grind it, or you can do it yourself in a food processor. Cut the chicken into 1" pieces and grind briefly. Do not overprocess, or the finished product will be mushy. Use the ground chicken within 1 day, or freeze it.

1. Prepare and preheat grill. In small skillet, heat olive oil over medium heat. Add onion and leek; cook and stir until tender, about 5 minutes. Add carrot; cook and stir another 2 minutes.

2. Remove from heat and transfer mixture to a large bowl. Add crumbled bread, mustard, salt, cayenne pepper, chili powder, and cumin; mix well. Add chicken; mix gently but thoroughly with hands.

3. Form into 4 patties; chill for 30 minutes. Grill patties 6" from medium coals, turning once, 5-6 minutes per side, or until internal temperature registers 165°F. Serve immediately.

SERVES 4

Calories: 290 | Carbohydrates: 14g | Fat: 16g | Sodium: 580mg | Fiber: 2g

Lemon Chicken Drumettes

Chicken wings are separated into 3 joints. Drumettes are the top joint of the wing and are like miniature drumsticks. They may be purchased precut, or the whole wing may be separated at the joints.

INGREDIENTS

4 pounds chicken drumettes

Salt and freshly ground black pepper to taste

1¼ cups water, divided

¼ cup orange juice

2 tablespoons grated fresh ginger

3 tablespoons vegetable oil

5 cloves garlic, finely chopped

1 cup very finely chopped fresh cilantro (about 3 bunches)

1 or 2 fresh jalapeño peppers, seeded and very finely chopped (according to taste)

2 teaspoons ground cumin

1 teaspoon ground coriander seeds

1 teaspoon salt

Lemon wedges for garnish (optional)

1. Preheat oven to 500°F. Line 2 baking sheets with aluminum foil.

2. Cut off the tips from the wings to make drumettes if necessary. Arrange the drumettes on the foil, trying not to overlap them. Season with salt and pepper. Place the baking pans on the top rack of the oven until brown, about 5 minutes. Turn the drumettes over and return to the oven to brown for another 3 minutes. Transfer the drumettes to paper towels and set aside, saving the pans.

3. Bring ¼ cup of water to a boil; stir in the orange juice. Combine this mixture with the ginger and 1 cup of water in a blender or food processor; purée to a smooth consistency.

4. In a large heavy skillet, heat the oil over medium-high heat. Add the garlic and cook until softened, about 2 minutes (be careful not to burn the garlic; reduce the heat if necessary). Reduce the heat and stir in the cilantro, jalapeños, cumin, coriander,

Lemon Chicken Drumettes

(continued)

Handling Raw Poultry

Raw poultry can carry salmonella bacteria. To prevent cross-contamination between raw meat and food that isn't going to be cooked, always thoroughly wash the cutting board, knife, and other utensils in hot, soapy water after handling raw poultry. If possible, use a separate cutting board and knife altogether for raw poultry.

and salt. Add the orange-ginger mixture to the pan; stir to mix. Turn up the heat, bring to a boil, and reduce the liquid until the sauce is thick, like salsa. Adjust seasoning to taste.

5. To serve, arrange the drumettes on a serving platter and top with the warm sauce. Garnish with lemon wedges surrounding the drumettes. Serve warm or cold.

SERVES 10

Calories: 340 | Carbohydrates: 2g | Fat: 20g | Sodium: 150mg | Fiber: 0g

Brined Grilled Chicken

Brining adds great flavor to chicken breasts and keeps them exceptionally moist. Great off the grill or cold in a picnic salad.

INGREDIENTS

6 bone-in, skin-on chicken breasts

3 tablespoons salt

2 tablespoons sugar

6 cups water, divided

2 tablespoons lemon juice

4 cloves garlic, minced

2 shallots, minced

1 teaspoon dried oregano leaves

¼ teaspoon cayenne pepper

3 tablespoons gluten-free tomato paste

2 tablespoons olive oil

1. Place chicken breasts, skin-side down, in large glass baking dish.

2. In medium bowl, combine salt and sugar. Add 1 cup of the water; stir to dissolve salt and sugar. Add 2 cups more water; mix.

3. Pour over chicken breasts; add remaining 3 cups water. Cover and refrigerate 3–4 hours.

4. When ready to cook, prepare and preheat grill.

5. In small bowl, combine remaining ingredients and mix well.

6. Remove chicken from brine; discard brine. Loosen skin from chicken breasts and rub half of the garlic mixture onto the flesh. Smooth skin back over chicken.

7. Rub remaining garlic mixture over chicken skin. Let chicken stand for 15 minutes.

Brined Grilled Chicken

(continued)

About Chicken Breasts

A whole chicken breast consists of two halves joined by cartilage. When a recipe calls for a chicken breast, technically it means half of a whole breast. You can buy them already split, or split them yourself to save a bit of money. If you buy bone-in breasts, you can remove the meat from the bone; save the bones to make chicken stock.

8. Place skin-side down on grill, 6" from medium coals. Cover and grill 8 minutes, then turn. Cover and grill 5 minutes longer, then check chicken.

9. Rearrange pieces to different parts of your grill, cover, and grill 7–9 minutes longer, or until meat thermometer registers 170°F.

SERVES 6

Calories: 340 | Carbohydrates: 11g | Fat: 18g |
Sodium: 3650mg | Fiber: <1g

Stuffed Cherry Tomatoes

You can flavor the basic filling any way you'd like: Add jalapeño peppers, chopped toasted nuts, tiny shrimp, cooked ground ham, or pepperoni.

INGREDIENTS

2 pints cherry tomatoes

1 cup soy-yogurt cheese

⅓ cup eggless mayonnaise

1 tablespoon gluten-free prepared horseradish

1 tablespoon lemon juice

¼ cup finely chopped ripe olives

⅓ cup chopped flat-leaf parsley

¼ cup chopped cilantro

Curly leaf parsley for garnish

1. Cut the top off each cherry tomato. Using a small serrated spoon or melon scoop, remove pulp and discard. Put tomatoes upside down on paper towel-lined plates to drain.

2. In small bowl, combine remaining ingredients; mix well to blend. Spoon or pipe filling into each cherry tomato.

3. To serve, place curly leaf parsley on a serving plate and arrange tomatoes on top. Cover with plastic wrap and chill at least 1 hour before serving. Bright and fun for any outdoor event.

YIELDS 24 APPETIZERS

Calories: 30 | Carbohydrates: 2g | Fat: 1.5g | Sodium: 110mg | Fiber: 0g

Chicken, Apple, Celery, and Nut Salad

If you ever wonder what to do with leftover chicken, or how to use chicken breasts for a quick lunch or snack, this fills the bill. It is a fine afterschool snack or quick lunch. And, you aren't filling your family with sugar.

INGREDIENTS

1 cup low-fat mayonnaise

1 teaspoon sweet-and-sour mustard

Salt and pepper to taste

½ teaspoon Splenda

½ teaspoon freshly squeezed lime juice

½ teaspoon curry powder, or to taste

¾ pound cooked chicken, diced

½ cup fresh apple, cored and diced

¼ cup white onion, minced

¼ cup celery, diced small

¼ cup peanuts, chopped

Optional garnish: 1 cup green grapes or raisins

Whisk the first six ingredients together in a bowl. When well mixed, stir in the rest of the items. Can be served immediately or chilled and served later.

YIELDS 2¾ CUPS;
SERVING SIZE 2 TABLESPOONS

Calories: 70 | Carbohydrates: 2g | Fat: 5g | Sodium: 90mg | Fiber: 0g

Grilled Vegetable Salad

*The pretty look of this dish will draw your child—
and your cookout company—right to it.*

INGREDIENTS

Salt and freshly ground pepper
   to taste

3 Japanese eggplants, halved

4 medium zucchini, trimmed and
   quartered lengthwise

2 yellow peppers, quartered and
   cored, seeds and membranes
   removed

6 plum tomatoes, cored and
   halved lengthwise

½ cup olive oil

Juice of ½ lemon

½ cup freshly grated Parmesan
   cheese

3 cups romaine lettuce

½ cup arugula

Lemon-herb dressing, to taste

1. Heat a grill to medium-high. Salt and pepper the vegetables on both sides. Whisk the oil and lemon juice together; brush the vegetables on both sides.

2. Grill for about 3 minutes per side, looking for grill marks on the eggplant and zucchini. Sprinkle with cheese.

3. Serve over the greens. Dress the greens in lemon-herb dressing, if desired.

YIELDS 6 SERVINGS; SERVING SIZE 1 CUP

Does not include dressing:
Calories: 290 | Carbohydrates: 24g | Fat: 21g | Sodium: 125mg | Fiber: 11g

Use the Season's Best Tastes

Try grilling vegetables with sprigs of fresh mint, basil, or oregano. This is ideal for a late summer treat when everything is in season and gardens are bursting.

Lobster Salad

Most fish markets sell cooked lobster meat. It's expensive, but not as much work as cooking and shelling lobsters at home.

INGREDIENTS

1 cup low-fat mayonnaise

Juice of ½ lime

1 teaspoon curry powder

1 teaspoon Dijon mustard

Salt and freshly ground pepper to taste

1 tablespoon concentrated unsweetened pineapple juice

1 pound cooked lobster meat

2 cups bitter greens, such as arugula or watercress, rinsed and dried on paper towels

½ cup roasted peanuts for garnish

1. In a large bowl, whisk the mayonnaise, lime juice, curry powder, Dijon mustard, salt, pepper, and pineapple juice together. Gently fold in the cooked lobster meat.

2. Arrange the greens on serving plates. Spoon the salad over the greens and garnish with peanuts.

**YIELDS 4 SERVINGS;
SERVING SIZE ⅔ CUP SALAD**

Calories: 320 | Carbohydrates: 15g | Fat: 18g | Sodium: 990mg | Fiber: 2g

Isn't Lobster Expensive?

Not in recent years. The recession has driven down the price of lobster in many regions. Check with your local fish market on current prices. You may be surprised.

Dilled Shrimp Salad with Cucumbers

*Shrimp salad is very versatile and easy to make.
Frozen shrimp takes all the work out of making a great shrimp salad.*

INGREDIENTS

1 tablespoon fresh dill or 1 teaspoon dried dill weed

½ cup low-fat mayonnaise

¼ cup sugar-free, low-fat plain yogurt

Juice of 1 lemon

Salt and pepper to taste

Red pepper flakes to taste

1 teaspoon sweet Hungarian paprika

1 teaspoon Worcestershire sauce or Asian fish sauce

½ English cucumber, rinsed and diced

1 pound cooked shrimp (frozen and thawed is fine; fresh is better)

1. Mix the dill, mayonnaise, yogurt, lemon, salt, pepper, red pepper flakes, paprika, and Worcestershire sauce together in a bowl. Add the cucumber and shrimp. Toss gently to coat with dressing.

2. Serve chilled over your favorite greens.

**YIELDS 4 SERVINGS;
SERVING SIZE 1 CUP SALAD**

Calories: 180 | Carbohydrates: 8g | Fat: 6g | Sodium: 540mg | Fiber: 0g

Grilled Red Snapper with Basil Aioli

If snapper isn't available,
you can substitute salmon.

INGREDIENTS

Vegetable oil for oiling grill

4 (6-ounce) red snapper fillets

Salt and freshly ground black
  pepper

¼ cup chopped fresh parsley

¼ cup chopped fresh basil

1 tablespoon mayonnaise

3 tablespoons olive oil

¼ cup chili sauce

Yes, Kids Actually Like Fish!

You'll be surprised how much children love white fish, and snapper is no exception. Serve it up and watch them ask for more.

1. Prepare a charcoal grill or preheat a gas grill to high heat. Make sure the grill grate is clean and lightly oiled to prevent sticking.

2. Season each fillet with salt and pepper. In a food processor or blender, combine the parsley, basil, mayonnaise, and olive oil; blend until smooth. Brush each fillet with this sauce.

3. Place the brushed fillets on the grill. Grill on each side for about 4 minutes, or until done. Serve immediately with the chili sauce on the side.

SERVES 4

Calories: 300 | Carbohydrates: 4g | Fat: 15g | Sodium: 320mg | Fiber: 0g

Roasted Vidalia Onions

This dish goes great with any grilled meat or fish.

INGREDIENTS

Vegetable oil for oiling grill

4 Vidalia or other sweet onions, peeled and cut in half crosswise

3 tablespoons olive oil

2 tablespoons balsamic vinegar

Salt and freshly ground black pepper to taste

2 strips bacon, cut into 8 pieces

Onions Can Stand on Their Own

Who says onions cannot be good alone or sans frying? See if these sweet summer specialties don't make onions a whole new treat for your kids.

1. Prepare a charcoal grill or preheat a gas grill to high. Make sure the grill grate is clean and lightly oiled to prevent sticking.

2. Place each onion half, cut-side up, in a 10" square of foil. Drizzle the onions with the oil and vinegar; season with salt and pepper. Turn the onions cut-side down. Place a piece of bacon on top of each onion. Fold the foil into packets.

3. Grill the onions for about 25 minutes, or until they are tender and slightly charred. Allow the onions to cool in their packets for 15 minutes.

4. Remove the onions, discarding the bacon but reserving the juices. Serve warm or at room temperature and drizzle the juices over the top.

SERVES 8

Calories: 110 | Carbohydrates: 9g | Fat: 8g | Sodium: 50mg | Fiber: 1g

Classic Coleslaw

No cookout is complete without coleslaw.
This one goes easy on carbs.

INGREDIENTS

2 cups mayonnaise

4 teaspoons sugar (or sugar
   substitute)

1½ teaspoons dry mustard

4 tablespoons white wine vinegar

8 cups shredded red or green
   cabbage

1 carrot, grated

1 onion, cut into a small dice

Salt and freshly ground black
   pepper to taste

In a large mixing bowl, whisk together the mayonnaise, sugar, mustard, and vinegar. Add the remaining ingredients; mix well to coat. Refrigerate for at least 1 hour before serving.

SERVES 10

Calories: 350 | Carbohydrates: 7g | Fat: 35g | Sodium: 260mg | Fiber: 2g

Marinated Beefsteak Tomatoes

*Kids will love these tomatoes with just about anything—
use as a garnish for burgers or serve with anything grilled.*

INGREDIENTS

3 tablespoons aged balsamic
   vinegar

2 tablespoons extra-virgin olive oil

Salt and freshly ground black
   pepper to taste

1 tablespoon chopped fresh
   parsley

1 tablespoon chopped fresh basil

1 large ripe beefsteak tomato, cut
   into ½" slices

In a medium-size bowl, whisk together
the vinegar, olive oil, salt, pepper, parsley, and basil. Add the tomato slices;
marinate for 1 hour before serving.
Best served at room temperature.

SERVES 2

Calories: 170 | Carbohydrates: 12g | Fat: 14g |
Sodium: 10mg | Fiber: 1g

Choosing Tomatoes

Commercial tomatoes are
grown more for shelf life than
for flavor. It is better to substitute canned roma tomatoes
than to use mushy fresh tomatoes. The best tomatoes are
fresh grown in your backyard
or purchased from your local
farmers' market.

CHAPTER 10

Super Snacks

Hot Hot Dogs GF

This is a really great way to serve hot dogs to people on a gluten-free diet. Turning them into a spread is an exciting twist.

INGREDIENTS

3 hot dogs, grilled, broiled, or boiled

2 teaspoons Dijon mustard

2 teaspoons chopped onion

2 teaspoons green or red relish

1 recipe Chickpea Crepes (see page 169)

1. Prepare a cookie sheet with nonstick spray. Preheat the oven to 350°F.

2. Mix the hot dogs, mustard, onion, and relish in a food processor.

3. Spread a teaspoon of the mixture on one quarter of each crepe; fold in half, then in quarters.

4. Bake for about 10 minutes, until hot. Serve with plenty of mustard on the side.

SERVES 6–8

Calories: 130 | Carbohydrates: 8g | Fat: 8.5g | Sodium: 570mg | Fiber: 0g

Baked Potato Chips

The nutritional allowance for this recipe allows for the teaspoon of olive oil. Even though you just spritz the potatoes with oil, remember that chips have more surface area than fries do.

INGREDIENTS

1 small white potato (3 ounces)

1 teaspoon olive oil

Sea salt and freshly ground black pepper to taste (optional)

Cut the Fat!

Eliminate the oil (and thus the fat exchange) in these Baked Potato Chips by using butter-flavored or olive oil cooking spray instead.

1. Preheat oven to 400°F.

2. Wash, peel, and thinly slice the potatoes. Wrap the slices in a paper towel to remove any excess moisture.

3. Spread the potatoes on a baking sheet treated with nonstick spray; spritz them with olive oil. Bake 10–15 minutes, depending on how crisp you prefer your fries. Season the potatoes with salt and pepper.

SERVES 1

Calories: 100 | Carbohydrates: 15g | Fat: 4.5g | Sodium: 30mg | Fiber: 1g

Sweet Potato Crisps

*There's a risk that these sweet potato strips will caramelize
and burn, so check them often while cooking.*

INGREDIENTS

1 small sweet potato or yam

1 teaspoon olive oil

Sea salt and freshly ground black
pepper to taste (optional)

1. Preheat oven to 400°F. Scrub the sweet potato and pierce the flesh several times with a fork. Place on a microwave-safe plate; microwave for 5 minutes on high. Remove from the microwave and wrap the sweet potato in aluminum foil. Set aside for 5 minutes.

2. Remove the foil, peel the potato, and cut it into French fries. Spread the fries on a baking sheet treated with nonstick spray; spritz with the olive oil. Bake 10–15 minutes, or until crisp. Check them often while cooking to ensure burning doesn't occur, lowering the oven temperature if necessary. Season with salt and pepper, if desired.

SERVES 2

Calories: 80 | Carbohydrates: 17g | Fat: 2.5g |
Sodium: 25mg | Fiber: 2g

Apple-Cheddar Melts on Pita Toast

A nice crisp apple is essential for this snack so that it won't turn mushy in the oven. Granny Smiths work well in this recipe, as do Empire and Ginger Gold apples.

INGREDIENTS

1 large whole-wheat pita bread

4 slices tart apple

4 slices Cheddar cheese, cut to fit the apple

The Pros of Wheat Pita

Whole-wheat pita bread stands up well to toasting and has a nutty and delicious flavor. You can also stuff it with any number of goodies and then bake it. Try pita toast instead of crackers as bases for various snacks.

1. Preheat the broiler to 400°F. Toast one side of the pita. Cut in quarters.

2. Stack an apple slice and cheese slice on the untoasted side of each pita piece. Place back under the broiler until cheese melts.

MAKES 4 SNACKS

Calories: 170 | Carbohydrates: 12g | Fat: 10g | Sodium: 260mg | Fiber: 2g

Peach Melba Smoothie

This pretty and delicious breakfast smoothie is a takeoff on the classic dessert Peach Melba.

INGREDIENTS

2 fresh, ripe peaches, peeled and sliced, or 1 cup frozen peaches

1 teaspoon lemon juice

1 cup plain yogurt

2 tablespoons sugar-free raspberry jam or jelly

2 teaspoons Splenda

1 teaspoon pure vanilla extract

1 cup crushed ice or ice chips

Fresh raspberries for garnish

Place all ingredients but the raspberries into blender. Blend until smooth. Pour into frosty glasses and garnish with a few raspberries on top of each smoothie.

YIELDS 2 SERVINGS;
SERVING SIZE 1 FOAMING CUP

Calories: 150 | Carbohydrates: 27g | Fat: 4.5g | Sodium: 55mg | Fiber: 2g

Grilled Pineapple

This is best cooked outdoors on a gas or charcoal grill.
Serve it with sugar-free ice cream or sorbet.

INGREDIENTS

4 thick slices fresh pineapple, core
   and skin removed

2 tablespoon butter, melted

2 tablespoons Splenda

1. Set your grill at medium-high or wait until the coals turn white. Brush both sides of the pineapple rings with melted butter.

2. Sprinkle with Splenda. Grill until you see grill marks; turn. Grill for a few more minutes.

YIELDS 4 SERVINGS;
SERVING SIZE 1 PIECE OF PINEAPPLE

Calories: 80 | Carbohydrates: 8g | Fat: 6g |
Sodium: 0mg | Fiber: <1g

Kiwi Balls with Frosted Strawberries

*Fixing a sweet and tasty icing for the berries makes
a very pretty and delicious presentation.*

INGREDIENTS

1 tablespoon Splenda

1 teaspoon cornstarch

½ teaspoon vanilla extract

1 teaspoon freshly squeezed
   lemon juice

1 tablespoon cold water

2 kiwi fruit, halved

12 medium-sized strawberries,
   hulled and halved

Do I Really Need a Mellon Baller?

Every kitchen needs two tiny
implements—a melon baller
and a grapefruit spoon. The
melon baller scoops up tiny
tastes of all sorts of goodies.
The grapefruit spoon has a
sharp point and serrated
edges and is excellent for cutting out the insides of many
other foods.

1. Whisk the Splenda, cornstarch,
   vanilla extract, lemon juice, and
   water together to make frosting. Set
   aside.

2. Use a melon baller to make balls of
   the kiwi fruit. Put kiwis and strawberries into a bowl.

3. Take a heavy-duty plastic bag and
   cut a tiny piece from the corner.
   Spoon the frosting mixture into the
   bag and drizzle over the fruit.

4. Chill and serve.

YIELDS 4 SERVINGS; SERVING SIZE ¼ CUP

Calories: 40 | Carbohydrates: 10g | Fat: 0g |
Sodium: 0mg | Fiber: 2g ‾

Pepper and Cheese Crackers

These little crackers are crisp and flaky, with an excellent spicy flavor. Serve them with hot soup for a satisfying lunch.

INGREDIENTS

½ cup butter, softened

1 tablespoon vegetable oil

2 tablespoons gluten-free mustard

1½ cups shredded sharp Cheddar cheese

2½ cups Gluten-Free, Soy-Free Baking Mix (page 47)

½ teaspoon freshly ground black pepper

⅛ teaspoon cayenne pepper

¼ cup 1% milk

1. Preheat oven to 400°F. In large bowl, combine butter, oil, mustard, and Cheddar cheese; mix. Add Baking Mix, pepper, and cayenne pepper; mix until crumbly. Add enough milk to make a firm, slightly crumbly dough.

2. Place dough on work surface; gently knead about 15 times. For each cracker, make three ½" diameter balls of dough and place them in a stack. Flatten each stack with hands to make 1 thin circle of dough. Place on Silpat-lined cookie sheets; prick with a fork. Repeat with remaining dough.

3. Bake 6–8 minutes, or until golden brown around edges. Carefully remove to wire rack to cool.

YIELDS 36 CRACKERS

Calories: 70 | Carbohydrates: 6g | Fat: 4.5g | Sodium: 40mg | Fiber: 0g

Strawberry Meringues

These pink, chewy, crunchy cookies are a great snack.

INGREDIENTS

3 egg whites

⅛ teaspoon cream of tartar

⅛ teaspoon salt

½ cup sugar

¼ cup gluten-free powdered sugar

½ teaspoon gluten-free strawberry extract

1 tablespoon organic gluten-free strawberry syrup

½ cup hard gluten-free strawberry-flavored candies, finely crushed

Yummy Yes, but You Still Need to Count

Even with low, low-carb foods it is important to pay attention to how much is being eaten. Carbs do add up, so be careful to keep track even of yummy low-carb treats.

1. Preheat oven to 350°F. Line a cookie sheet with parchment paper and set aside.

2. In large bowl, beat egg whites, cream of tartar, and salt until soft peaks form. Gradually add sugar, beating until stiff. Beat in powdered sugar, strawberry extract, and strawberry syrup until well blended.

3. Fold in crushed candies. Drop by tablespoons onto prepared cookie sheet. Bake 25–30 minutes, or until cookies are dry to the touch. Let cool 5 minutes, then carefully peel off paper; cool completely on wire rack. Store covered at room temperature.

YIELDS 24 COOKIES

Calories: 45 | Carbohydrates: 10g | Fat: 0g | Sodium: 20mg | Fiber: 0g

Pepperoni Chips

These little crunch treats are quite addictive and store well, even at room temperature. Make them in large portions and keep them around.

INGREDIENTS

1 (8-ounce) package sliced pepperoni

Coarse ground pepper to taste

1. Preheat oven to 350°F.

2. Place pepperoni slices in single layer on nonstick baking sheet. Bake 10–12 minutes, or until crispy.

3. Transfer to paper towel to cool and absorb grease.

4. Season with pepper to taste (optional).

SERVES 8

Calories: 140 | Carbohydrates: 0g | Fat: 13g | Sodium: 520mg | Fiber: 0g

Sweet-and-Spicy Toasted Nut Mix

This is very easy and delicious,
and it keeps for a couple of weeks in an airtight container.

INGREDIENTS

¼ cup Splenda

½ cup unsalted butter, melted

2 teaspoons freshly ground black
    pepper

1 teaspoon coarse salt

½ pound blanched almonds

½ pound walnut halves

1. Preheat the oven to 400°F. Prepare a baking sheet with parchment paper or nonstick spray. Whisk the first four ingredients together in a large bowl.

2. Stir in the nuts. Turn until all are covered. Spread on the baking sheet. Bake for 10–12 minutes, checking often.

3. Cool at room temperature; store in tightly covered container.

YIELDS 18 SERVINGS; SERVING SIZE 8 NUTS

Calories: 200 | Carbohydrates: 5g | Fat: 20g | Sodium: 135mg | Fiber: 2g

Pita Toast with Herbs and Cheese

*These pita toast snacks are an easy alternative to traditional appetizers.
They work equally well as after school snacks
for kids and starters for a cocktail party.*

INGREDIENTS

1 whole wheat pita

2 tablespoons cream cheese, at
room temperature

2 teaspoons Gorgonzola cheese,
at room temperature

2 sprigs fresh parsley, minced

2 tablespoons chives, minced

Salt and pepper to taste

1. Toast the pita and cut in fourths.

2. Using a fork, mix the rest of the
   ingredients together in a small bowl.
   Spread on pitas and serve.

MAKES 4 SNACKS

Calories: 70 | Carbohydrates: 9g | Fat: 3.5g |
Sodium: 125mg | Fiber: 1g

Creamy Spiced Dip for Crudités

*This recipe is a tasty way to get the right amounts
of vitamin-loaded veggies into your diet.*

INGREDIENTS

½ cup low-fat mayonnaise

½ cup low-fat sour cream

¼ cup fresh parsley, chopped

4 scallions, chopped

1 teaspoon curry powder

1 tablespoon fresh lime juice

Salt and hot red pepper flakes to
taste

Pulse all ingredients in the food processor or blender. Serve cold with a selection of raw vegetables.

MAKES 1 CUP: 4 SERVINGS PER CUP

Calories: 100 | Carbohydrates: 7g | Fat: 8g |
Sodium: 280mg | Fiber: 0g

Dip for Fresh Fruit

This is excellent with slices of apple, pineapple, or pear.
Enjoy with any seasonal fruit.

INGREDIENTS

4 ounces low-fat cream cheese

4 ounces low-fat cottage cheese

1 teaspoon sugar substitute, or to
taste

1 teaspoon freshly ground white
pepper

2 tablespoons cider vinegar or
lemon juice

½ teaspoon salt, or to taste

Blend all ingredients in the blender.
Serve chilled.

MAKES 1½ CUPS: SERVING SIZE ½ CUP

Calories: 120 | Carbohydrates: 5g | Fat: 7g |
Sodium: 710mg | Fiber: 0g

Dip-itty DO!

Kids love dip! If you are looking for a way to get healthy
fruit and veggies into a daily
plan, add some of these health-
wise dips and watch them get
devoured.

Honey Raisin Bars

This recipe makes crisp cookies. If you like chewier cookies or need to cut the fat in your diet, you can substitute applesauce, plums, prunes, or mashed banana for the sunflower oil.

INGREDIENTS

½ cup unbleached all-purpose flour

¼ teaspoon baking soda

⅛ teaspoon sea salt

¼ teaspoon cinnamon

¾ cup quick-cooking oatmeal

1 egg white, slightly beaten

2½ tablespoons sunflower oil

¼ cup honey

¼ cup skim milk

½ teaspoon vanilla

½ cup golden raisins

12–15 Gram Perfection

Any tasty, cookie-like snack that only "costs" you about 12g of carb is a sure thing, be it for snack time at school, at home, or on the run. It's also the perfect amount to treat a low blood sugar.

1. Preheat oven to 350°F. Sift the flour, soda, salt, and cinnamon together into a bowl; stir in the oatmeal.

2. In another bowl, mix the slightly beaten egg white with the oil, honey, milk, vanilla, and raisins. Add the flour mixture to liquid ingredients. Drop by teaspoons onto cookie sheets treated with nonstick spray. Bake 12–15 minutes. (Longer baking time will result in crispier cookies.) Cool on a baking rack.

3. For cookie bars, spread the mixture in an even layer on a piece of parchment paper placed on the cookie sheet; bake 15–18 minutes. Cool slightly, then use a sharp knife or pizza cutter to slice into 18 equal pieces (6 cuts downward, 3 across).

SERVES 18

Calories: 70 | Carbohydrates: 12g | Fat: 2g | Sodium: 40mg | Fiber: <1g

Guacamole

*Use guacamole as a topping or accompaniment
to grilled meats and poultry.*

INGREDIENTS

4 tomatillos, peeled, rinsed, and
  finely chopped

¼ medium onion, finely chopped

¼ cup coarsely chopped fresh
  cilantro

1 or 2 jalapeño peppers, seeded
  and finely chopped

1 clove garlic, minced

2 small avocados, peeled and
  pitted

1 tomato, cut into a small dice

1 tablespoon lime juice

Salt and freshly ground black
  pepper to taste

In a medium-size bowl, combine all the ingredients. Use the back of a fork to mash all of the ingredients until puréed but still slightly chunky. Best served the same day. Keep the avocado pit in the guacamole to prevent it from browning.

SERVES 10 (MAKES 2½ CUPS)

Calories: 70 | Carbohydrates: 5g | Fat: 5g |
Sodium: 0mg | Fiber: 4g

Southern Twist

You may want to go regional when shopping for this recipe. Florida avocados contain about 30 percent less fat than the traditional Hass avocados.

Creamy Dill Dip

Use baby carrots, tiny celery sticks, bell pepper strips,
and cauliflower florets for dippers.

INGREDIENTS

1 cup soy-yogurt cheese

¼ cup low-fat mayonnaise

¼ cup finely chopped green onion

2 tablespoons chopped flat-leaf
  parsley

1 tablespoon dried dill weed

½ teaspoon lemon pepper

½ teaspoon gluten-free seasoned
  salt

In small bowl, combine all ingredients; mix well to blend. Cover and chill 2–3 hours before serving.

YIELDS 1½ CUPS;
SERVING SIZE 2 TABLESPOONS

Calories: 40 | Carbohydrates: 2g | Fat: 1.5g | Sodium: 280mg | Fiber: 0g

Chickpea Crepes

These are so versatile—you can stuff and fold them or roll and stuff them, as you would cannelloni or manicotti, for a meal.

INGREDIENTS

1¼ cups cold water

1 egg

1 teaspoon Tabasco or other red pepper sauce

1 cup chickpea flour

1 teaspoon salt

1 teaspoon garlic powder (optional)

Vegetable or olive oil for frying

Stuffings and Spreads

Making spreads and stuffings for any number of things is a great way to use leftovers. You can take a chunk of leftover Brie cheese and put it in the food processor with some chopped onion and a bit of butter or margarine and have a whole new experience. Leftover chicken is excellent for making many different spreads, filling for stuffed celery, or a little sandwich.

1. Place the water, egg, and Tabasco in a blender or food processor. Pulse, slowly adding the flour. Stop and scrape down the sides.

2. Mix in the salt and garlic powder. Heat a nonstick pan over medium-high heat and add a teaspoon of olive or vegetable oil.

3. Pour about 2 ounces of batter into the pan, tipping it quickly to spread the batter. Fry for about 3 minutes, or until the edges are crisp. Flip carefully, and when golden, place on waxed paper or parchment to cool.

4. Fold or form into tubes. Stuff with filling of your choice.

MAKES ENOUGH FOR 8 SNACKS

Calories: 50 | Carbohydrates: 7g | Fat: 1.5g | Sodium: 300mg | Fiber: 0g

CHAPTER 11

Sick-Day Recipes

Herb Crackers

*These delicious crackers are totally free of sugar and have no trans fats,
unlike many commercially manufactured crackers.
They are very easy to make and delicious!*

INGREDIENTS

1½ cups all-purpose flour

½ cup whole-wheat flour

½ teaspoon salt

2 teaspoons fresh rosemary, finely
chopped

1 teaspoon garlic powder

5 tablespoons extra-virgin olive
oil, divided

¼ cup low-fat milk (more if
needed to moisten dough)

1 tablespoon dried oregano
leaves

1 tablespoon coarse sea salt

Nibbling Is Okay, Done Right

Kids with diabetes need to at
least nibble all day long to give
their bodies fuel to match their
insulin input. Easy-to-digest
crackers are a great bet.

1. Preheat the oven to 425°F. In a large
   bowl, thoroughly combine the flours,
   salt, rosemary, and garlic powder.
   Stir in 4 tablespoons of olive oil.

2. Work the dough with your fingers or
   a food processor until it is the consistency of oatmeal. Stir milk in gradually, adding enough to make the
   dough hold together firmly.

3. Line a cookie sheet with parchment
   paper. Roll out the dough into a 12"
   × 16" rectangle.

4. Wrap the dough around the rolling
   pin and then unwrap it onto parchment paper. Cut into 1" strips. Cut
   across strips to make 1" squares.

5. Brush the tops of dough squares
   with remaining tablespoon of olive
   oil. Sprinkle with oregano and sea
   salt. Bake for 15 minutes, until lightly
   browned. Cool. Store in an airtight
   container. Crackers will last a week.

YIELDS 48 CRACKERS;
SERVING SIZE 4 CRACKERS

Calories: 130 | Carbohydrates: 16g | Fat: 6g |
Sodium: 680mg | Fiber: 1g

Herb Mélange

You can use some dried herbs in this recipe, but make sure you opt for fresh basil and parsley. Also use medium or whipping cream, not heavy cream. You can add more if you want a white soup, but it's not necessary.

INGREDIENTS

1 tablespoon rice flour

2 tablespoons cold water

2 tablespoons olive oil

4 cloves garlic, chopped

1 small onion, peeled and chopped

2 tablespoons fresh rosemary or 1 tablespoon dried rosemary

2 tablespoons fresh thyme or 1 teaspoon dried thyme

½ cup fresh basil leaves, stemmed and torn

½ cup fresh Italian flat-leaf parsley, chopped

Red pepper flakes to taste

Salt and freshly ground black pepper to taste

6 cups chicken broth

1 teaspoon soy sauce

½ cup medium or whipping cream

3 tablespoons freshly snipped chives for garnish

1. Combine flour and water; stir to make a smooth paste.

2. Heat the oil in a large pot. Sauté the garlic and onion. When they are soft, blend in the flour, herbs, red pepper, salt, and pepper. Whisk in the chicken broth and soy sauce.

3. Blend the soup in the blender in batches. When puréed, add the cream. Serve hot or chilled.

YIELDS 8 SERVINGS; SERVING SIZE 6 OUNCES

Calories: 97 | Carbohydrates: 5g | Fat: 8g | Sodium: 420mg | Fiber: <1g |

Don't Do Sick Days Alone

Any time your child has a sick day, you should at least check in with his medical team. Look to them for advice on when to cut back on insulin or add carbs and how often to check blood sugars and ketones. You don't need to go it alone!

Chicken Apple Sandwiches

Grilled sandwiches make an excellent quick lunch.
You can keep this filling in the refrigerator, covered, for up to 3 days.

INGREDIENTS

2 cups cubed cooked chicken

1 Granny Smith apple, peeled and diced

1 cup shredded carrot

½ cup vegan mayonnaise

½ teaspoon dried thyme leaves

⅛ teaspoon pepper

1 cup shredded dairy-free, vegan mozzarella cheese

8 slices gluten-free bread

2 tablespoons olive oil

1. In medium bowl, combine chicken, apple, and carrot; mix gently. Add mayonnaise, thyme, and pepper; mix well. Stir in cheese.

2. Make sandwiches using two slices of bread for each. Brush outsides of sandwiches with the olive oil.

3. Cook in covered preheated skillet 5–6 minutes, turning once, or in a panini maker 3–4 minutes, until bread is toasted and filling is hot. Serve immediately.

SERVES 4

Calories: 560 | Carbohydrates: 45g | Fat: 27g | Sodium: 680mg | Fiber: 2g

Graham Crackers

Making your own graham crackers is a fun family project (even on a sick day!). Even small children can help measure the sugar and Baking Mix.

INGREDIENTS

1¼ cups Gluten-Free, Soy-Free Baking Mix (page 47)

1 cup brown-rice flour

⅓ cup brown sugar

½ teaspoon baking soda

1 teaspoon gluten-free baking powder

½ teaspoon salt

½ teaspoon cinnamon

⅓ cup coconut oil

3 tablespoons dairy-free vegan margarine

3 tablespoons honey

1 teaspoon gluten-free vanilla

¼ cup rice milk

2–4 tablespoons cold water

Baking with Care

When you're baking cookies and crackers, your oven temperature must be accurate for best results. Use an oven thermometer, and watch the cookies or crackers carefully as they bake, especially toward the end of baking time. You may need to rotate the cookie sheet or remove some of the pieces that test done before others.

1. In large bowl, combine Baking Mix, brown-rice flour, brown sugar, baking soda, baking powder, salt, and cinnamon; mix well with wire whisk.

2. In small saucepan, combine coconut oil, margarine, and honey. Heat over low heat, stirring frequently, until mixture is melted and smooth.

3. Add oil mixture to dry ingredients along with vanilla, rice milk, and 2 tablespoons cold water; mix until a dough forms. You may need to add more water or Baking Mix to make a firm dough. Cover and refrigerate dough 2–3 hours.

4. Preheat oven to 325°F. Roll out dough between sheets of waxed paper until it is ⅛" thick. Cut into 2" squares and place 1" apart on Silpat-lined cookie sheets.

5. Prick crackers with a fork. Bake 20–30 minutes, or until crackers are deep golden brown, removing some of them if they start looking too dark.

YIELDS ABOUT 48 CRACKERS

Calories: 60 | Carbohydrates: 8g | Fat: 2.5g | Sodium: 45mg | Fiber: 1g

Cinnamon Crisps

The combination of flours and starch in these cookies
makes them delicate and crisp at the same time.

INGREDIENTS

½ cup superfine rice flour

¼ cup honey

¼ cup vegetable oil

2 teaspoons gluten-free vanilla

2 tablespoons potato-starch flour

2 tablespoons tapioca flour

½ teaspoon xanthan gum

⅓ cup brown sugar

½ cup gluten-free rolled oats

¼ teaspoon salt

1 teaspoon cinnamon, divided

½ cup dried currants

2 tablespoons sugar

1. Preheat oven to 375°F. In small bowl, combine rice flour, honey, vegetable oil, and vanilla; mix well.

2. In food processor, combine potato-starch flour, tapioca flour, xanthan gum, brown sugar, and rolled oats. Process until fine, then stir in salt and ½ teaspoon cinnamon. Stir in rice flour mixture until a dough forms, then add currants.

3. Roll dough into ¾" balls. On plate, combine sugar with remaining ½ teaspoon cinnamon; mix well. Roll dough balls in cinnamon-sugar mixture; place on ungreased cookie sheet.

4. Flatten cookies with the bottom of a glass. Bake 11–15 minutes, or until cookies are light golden brown; remove from cookie sheet and cool completely on wire rack. Store tightly covered at room temperature.

YIELDS 24 COOKIES

Calories: 80 | Carbohydrates: 15g | Fat: 2.5g | Sodium: 25mg | Fiber: <1g

Bagel Chips

You can buy bagel chips in the supermarket, but they are usually so hard you could break your teeth. Try these instead!

INGREDIENTS

2 whole-wheat or pumpernickel
bagels

2 tablespoons olive oil (in spray
bottle if possible)

Garlic salt and pepper to taste

1. Thinly slice the bagels crosswise, discarding the tiny ends.

2. Spread the pieces on a baking sheet. Spray with olive oil and sprinkle with garlic salt and pepper.

3. Bake at 350°F for 10 minutes. Serve as crackers.

MAKES 12 CHIPS

Calories: 45 | Carbohydrates: 9g | Fat: 0g |
Sodium: 75mg | Fiber: 2g

Frozen Grapes

This snack is very sweet but not at all fattening.

INGREDIENTS

1 pound grapes, rinsed

2 teaspoons Splenda

Soothing and Yummy Works on Sick Days

On some sick days your medical team will tell you to just try to keep your child taking in at least tiny bits of carb at a time. These grapes are a fun—and soothing—way to do just that.

Prepare a cookie sheet with nonstick spray. Place the damp grapes on the cookie sheet, sprinkle with Splenda, and freeze. Use commercial lemon yogurt with no sugar as a dipping sauce for the frozen grapes.

YIELDS 1 POUND GRAPES; SERVING SIZE 4 OUNCES

Calories: 70 | Carbohydrates: 20g | Fat: 1g | Sodium: 0mg | Fiber: <1g

Blueberry Muffins

These muffins freeze beautifully, so make a double batch and reheat leftovers for a quick breakfast treat. Make extras when blueberries are in season, plentiful, and inexpensive.

INGREDIENTS

2 eggs

1 teaspoon salt

1 cup milk

1 tablespoon unsalted butter, melted

1½ cup whole-wheat flour

1 cups coarse cornmeal

1 tablespoon baking powder

½ cup Splenda

1 cup fresh or frozen blueberries, rinsed and dried

Juicy but Not Too Juicy

Make sure you dry fresh berries before you add them to muffin batter. If they are wet, the added moisture will throw off your recipe. If the berries are super juicy, you can always add more flour. Add it 1 tablespoon at a time and check it.

1. Preheat oven to 350°F.

2. Whisk the eggs, salt, milk, and butter together until light and fluffy. Stir in the flour, cornmeal, baking powder, and Splenda. Gently fold in the berries.

3. Prepare a muffin tin with nonstick spray. Fill each cup halfway with batter. Bake 15–20 minutes.

YIELDS 12 MUFFINS; SERVING SIZE 1 MUFFIN

Calories: 140 | Carbohydrates: 26g | Fat: 2.5g | Sodium: 340mg | Fiber: 3g

Fruit Salsa

You can also add additional seasonings to this recipe according to your individual tastes, including parsley, cilantro, sea salt, or cayenne pepper.

INGREDIENTS

½ of a cantaloupe

1 jalapeño or banana pepper

1 cup blackberries

1 small red or green bell pepper

1 medium-sized red onion

1 tablespoon lemon juice

Place all the ingredients in a food processor and process until well mixed. Do not overprocess; you want the salsa to remain somewhat chunky.

YIELDS ABOUT 2 CUPS;
SERVING SIZE 2 TABLESPOONS

Calories: 20 | Carbohydrates: 4g | Fat: 0g | Sodium: 0mg | Fiber: <1g

Frothy Orange Jewel

*If you don't have fresh orange juice on hand, you can substitute
1 tablespoon frozen orange juice concentrate and 3 tablespoons of water.*

INGREDIENTS

¼ cup fresh orange juice

1 cup skim milk

1½ teaspoons powdered sugar

½ teaspoon vanilla

1 or 2 ice cubes (optional)

Combine all the ingredients in a blender and process until mixed. Serve in a frosted glass.

SERVES 1

Calories: 130 | Carbohydrates: 23g | Fat: 0g | Sodium: 105mg | Fiber: 0g

Chicken Mushroom Tartlets

Tartlets are a great way to get kids to eat healthy. They are so fun to pop in a mouth, kids don't look at what's in it until they eat it—and like it.

INGREDIENTS

1 boneless, skinless chicken breast, diced

2 tablespoons flour

½ teaspoon salt

⅛ teaspoon pepper

1 tablespoon olive oil

1 onion, chopped

1 cup sliced button mushrooms

1 tablespoon lemon juice

½ teaspoon dried thyme leaves

¼ cup eggless mayonnaise

½ cup chopped cherry tomatoes

32 frozen mini tartlet shells

Tarts Are Just Baby Pies

You can sometimes find tartlet shells in the bakery or frozen foods aisle of the supermarket, but if you have a pie-crust recipe you like, use that to make the little shells. You can roll out the dough, cut into 2" rounds, and fit those in the miniature muffin cups, or roll the dough into ¾" balls and press into the muffin cups.

1. Preheat oven to 375°F. Toss chicken with flour, salt, and pepper. Heat olive oil in medium skillet. Add chicken; stir until thoroughly cooked, about 4–6 minutes. Remove chicken from skillet with slotted spoon and set aside in medium bowl.

2. Add onion to skillet; cook and stir until the edges begin to brown, about 8–10 minutes. Add mushrooms; cook and stir until tender, about 4–5 minutes longer. Remove half of this mixture to food processor; process until smooth and thick.

3. Add processed mixture to chicken in bowl along with unprocessed onion and mushrooms, along with lemon juice, thyme, mayonnaise, and tomatoes; stir well to mix. Fill each tartlet shell with about 2 teaspoons filling; place on cookie sheet.

4. Bake 9–14 minutes, or until filling is hot and shells are golden brown. Cool for 10 minutes, then serve.

YIELDS 32 TARTLETS

Calories: 150 | Carbohydrates: 20g | Fat: 7g | Sodium: 140mg | Fiber: 0g

Vegetable Broth

Vegetable broth can be fairly unflavored, but not this recipe!
Browning the onions and garlic first adds great caramelized flavor.
Just the right thing to sip on to stay hydrated on a sick day.

INGREDIENTS

2 tablespoons olive oil

2 onions, chopped

4 cloves garlic, chopped

4 carrots, sliced

3 stalks celery with leaves, chopped

5 tomatoes, chopped

1 teaspoon salt

¼ teaspoon pepper

¼ teaspoon ground cloves

1 bay leaf

9 cups water

Freezing Broth

All stocks and broths freeze very well. Cool the liquid completely, then skim off any fat that accumulates on the surface. Divide into 2-cup hard-sided freezer containers, leaving about 1" of headspace for expansion during freezing. Label the containers, seal, and freeze for up to 3 months. To use, let stand in refrigerator overnight to thaw.

1. In a large soup pot, heat olive oil over medium heat. Add onion and garlic; cook and stir until onion begins to brown, about 9–11 minutes. Add carrots; cook and stir 7–8 minutes longer, until onions are brown and carrots are tender.

2. Add remaining ingredients and stir to combine. Bring to a boil, then skim surface, reduce heat, and simmer 1–2 hours, or until liquid is slightly reduced and broth tastes rich.

3. Strain broth, pressing down on vegetables to extract all the juices. Store broth covered in refrigerator up to 3 days or freeze for longer storage.

YIELDS 6 CUPS; SERVING SIZE 1 CUP

Calories: 120 | Carbohydrates: 18g | Fat: 5g | Sodium: 450mg | Fiber: 4g

Lentil Soup with Winter Vegetables

This is a substantial soup that will help a sick child get some carbs into his system while still feeling soothed.

INGREDIENTS

½ pound bag red or yellow lentils

4 cups Vegetable Broth (page 183)

2 cups water

2 parsnips, peeled and chopped

2 carrots, peeled and chopped

2 white onions, chopped

4 cloves garlic, chopped

4 small bluenose turnips, peeled and chopped

½ pound deli baked ham, cut in cubes

Salt and pepper to taste

Put all ingredients in a soup kettle. Bring to a boil, cover, and simmer for 1 hour.

SERVES 4

Calories: 400 | Carbohydrates: 70g | Fat: 2g | Sodium: 1190mg | Fiber: 16g

CHAPTER 12

International Flavor, D-Kid's Style

A Taste of Italy Baked Fish

This dish is good served over couscous, orzo, pasta, rice, or steamed cabbage, or alongside polenta. Add veggies like those you'd use for pizza toppings—like chopped peppers or sliced mushrooms—to this dish.

INGREDIENTS

1 pound (16 ounces) cod fillets

1 (14½-ounce) can stewed tomatoes

¼ teaspoon dried minced onion

½ teaspoon dried minced garlic

¼ teaspoon dried basil

¼ teaspoon dried parsley

⅛ teaspoon dried oregano

⅛ teaspoon sugar

1 tablespoon grated Parmesan cheese

1. Preheat oven to 375°F. Rinse the cod with cold water and pat dry with paper towels.

2. In a 2- to 3-quart baking pan or casserole treated with nonstick cooking spray, combine all the ingredients *except* the fish; mix. Arrange the fillets over the tomato mixture, folding thin tail ends under to give the fillets an even thickness; spoon some of the tomato mixture over the fillets, if desired. For fillets about 1" thick, bake uncovered for 20–25 minutes, or until the fish is opaque and flaky.

SERVES 4

Calories: 130 | Carbohydrates: 6g | Fat: 1g | Sodium: 310mg | Fiber: 2g

Family Style Hungarian Goulash

"Sweet" paprika is made from a special breed of red peppers that are not hot. Hot paprika is made from red chili peppers. Adding just a bit of Splenda to the goulash (stew) will provide a lovely balance with the vinegar.

INGREDIENTS

2 tablespoons peanut oil, divided

1 tablespoon unsalted butter

3 yellow onions, peeled, cut into coarse dice

2 pounds stewing veal, boneless

1 tablespoon whole-wheat flour

1 teaspoon salt

½ teaspoon freshly ground black pepper, or to taste

1 tablespoon paprika

1 teaspoon Splenda

1 teaspoon caraway seeds

1 teaspoon dried marjoram leaves

1 tablespoon red wine vinegar

1 cup beef broth

1 cup tomato juice, no sugar added

1 cup sour cream (optional)

1. Preheat the oven to 325°F. Prepare a 2-quart casserole with nonstick spray. In a large frying pan over medium heat, combine 1 tablespoon of the oil and the butter. Add the onions; cook and stir until softened, but not browned.

2. Scrape the onions into the casserole. Add the second tablespoon of oil; stir in the veal. Brown the beef; add to the casserole with the onion.

3. Add all remaining ingredients but the sour cream, one at a time, stirring to blend. Cover casserole and bake for 2 hours, or until the veal is very tender. If the liquid dries out, add some more broth or tomato juice.

4. Just before serving, add the sour cream. Serve over noodles.

SERVES 6; SERVING SIZE 1 CUP

Calories: 610 | Carbohydrates: 12g | Fat: 41g | Sodium: 740mg | Fiber: 2g

Crispy Rice Balls

Fry these little balls as your guests arrive.
They're crisp and savory, with a tender center. If you aren't allergic to
cheese, try molding the rice around a tiny square of cheese before frying.

INGREDIENTS

1 cup medium-grain rice

2 cups water

1 tablespoon olive oil

½ cup minced onion

3 cloves garlic, minced

1 egg

½ teaspoon salt

⅛ teaspoon cayenne pepper

2 tablespoons prepared gluten-
  free horseradish

½ teaspoon dried thyme leaves

1 cup crushed puffed-rice cereal

1 cup vegetable oil

The Stickier Rices

Rice can be long grain, medium grain, or short grain. They differ in the amount and kind of starch they contain. Long-grain rice cooks up fluffier because it has less amylopectin, the starch that makes rice sticky. Medium-grain rice has more amylopectin, so it is stickier, suitable for rice balls.

1. In medium saucepan, combine rice and water. Bring to a boil over high heat, then reduce heat to low. Simmer 18–23 minutes, or until rice is tender and water is absorbed.

2. Meanwhile, heat olive oil over medium heat in medium skillet. Add onion; cook and stir until onion begins to brown, about 8–9 minutes. Stir in garlic for 1 minute, then stir the mixture into hot cooked rice. Let rice mixture cool for 30 minutes; add egg, salt, cayenne pepper, horseradish, and thyme.

3. Form mixture into 1" balls; roll in crushed cereal to coat.

4. Heat oil in heavy skillet over medium heat. Fry rice balls, turning carefully, until golden brown and crisp, about 4–5 minutes. Drain on paper towels and serve.

SERVES 8

Calories: 370 | Carbohydrates: 23g | Fat: 30g |
Sodium: 160mg | Fiber: <1g

Thai Chicken Stew with Vegetables in Coconut Cream

Asian flavorings can provide so many minimal, yet wonderful, additions to rather ordinary foods. This chicken stew is spicy and tastes very rich.

INGREDIENTS

2 cloves garlic, minced

1" fresh gingerroot, peeled and minced

2 tablespoons peanut oil

2 carrots, shredded

1 cup canned coconut cream

1 cup chicken broth

2 cups Napa cabbage, shredded

4 chicken breasts (about 5 ounces each) boneless and skinless, in bite-size pieces

¼ cup soy sauce

2 tablespoons Asian fish sauce

1 teaspoon Thai chili paste (red or green) or red hot pepper sauce

1 tablespoon sesame oil

½ cup scallions, greens chopped

¼ cup cilantro, chopped

1. Sauté the garlic and gingerroot in the peanut oil. Add the carrots, coconut cream, and chicken broth; simmer for 10 minutes. Add the cabbage, chicken, soy sauce, and Asian fish sauce.

2. Whisk in the chili paste. Stir in the sesame oil, scallions, and cilantro. Simmer for 20 minutes. Serve over rice.

SERVES 4

Calories: 440 | Carbohydrates: 15g | Fat: 25g | Sodium: 2060mg | Fiber: 4g

Gluten-Free Sweet Crepes

Crepes are very thin, unleavened pancakes.
You can fill these with sorbet, sautéed apples, or chocolate pudding.

INGREDIENTS

½ cup superfine rice flour

¼ cup brown-rice flour

¼ cup tapioca flour

½ teaspoon xanthan gum

2 tablespoons sugar

⅛ teaspoon salt

¾ cup vegan egg replacer

1 tablespoon vegetable oil

1 teaspoon gluten-free vanilla

4–6 tablespoons rice milk or soy milk

Get Kids into the Process

Meals that are fun to create— like crepes—are usually fun to eat, too. Make creating these unusual meals a family affair and your kids will be more willing to taste something new and different.

1. In food processor or blender, combine all ingredients except rice milk; process or blend until smooth. Add enough rice milk to make a thin batter. Let stand 5 minutes.

2. Heat a nonstick 6" skillet over medium heat. Brush with a bit of oil. Using a ½ cup measure, pour about ⅓ cup of the batter into the hot pan. Immediately lift and tilt the pan so the batter coats the bottom. Cook 2–3 minutes, or until crepe is set and slightly crisp; turn and cook 30 seconds on second side.

3. As the crepes are finished, place on kitchen towels to cool. Do not stack crepes or they will stick together. You can freeze these, separated by parchment paper or waxed paper, up to 2 months. To thaw, let stand at room temperature for 20–30 minutes.

YIELDS 12 CREPES

Calories: 70 | Carbohydrates: 13g | Fat: 1.5g | Sodium: 45mg | Fiber: 0g

Spanish Garlic-and-Sausage Soup

As with so many classic rustic dishes,
each Spanish village adds a distinctive touch to this classic soup,
and each cook adds his or her own favorite seasonings.

INGREDIENTS

2 tablespoons olive oil

1 teaspoon minced garlic

½ cup red onion

½ pound sugarless chorizo
  sausage, thinly sliced

6 cups chicken broth

1 cup fresh or canned diced
  tomatoes

1 teaspoon dried oregano

1 teaspoon Splenda

1 bunch Italian flat-leaf parsley

Salt or pepper to taste

1. Heat the olive oil in a large soup kettle. Add the garlic and onions; cook, stirring, over medium heat until the garlic has become a paste and the onions are translucent.

2. Stir in the rest of the ingredients. Taste before adding the salt and pepper; since the sausage contains sodium, you may not need any. Cover and simmer over low heat for 60 minutes. Serve hot.

YIELDS 8 SERVINGS; SERVING SIZE 8 OUNCES

Calories: 200 | Carbohydrates: 10g | Fat: 15g |
Sodium: 960mg | Fiber: 1g

Should Kids Stay Away from Spicy?

Not at all. Go easy at first, but developing a love of spices can be a great way to help a child learn to love foods without adding carbs.

Swedish Coffee Bread

*This braided bread is a sweet Scandinavian delicacy.
It is particularly popular around the holiday season.*

INGREDIENTS

1 ounce live yeast, crumbled

½ cup warm milk

½ cup unsalted butter

1 cup Splenda, divided

1 teaspoon salt

3 eggs, divided

½ cup cold milk

2 cups all-purpose flour

2 cups whole-wheat flour plus
   extra for sprinkling

1 tablespoon ground cardamom

1 tablespoon ground cinnamon

1 cup raisins without added sugar

1 cup chopped pecans or walnuts

1. In a small bowl, mix the yeast and warm milk. Set aside.

2. In a large bowl, mix the unsalted butter, ½ cup Splenda, and salt. Beat in 2 of the eggs and the cold milk. Stir in the yeast mixture. Set aside for 10 minutes; stir in the flours, mixing well.

3. Cover the bowl and let dough rise in a warm place for 60 minutes.

4. Sprinkle a flat surface with whole-wheat flour and roll the dough out onto it. Knead the dough until it is smooth and elastic. Roll into a long rope, about 18" long and ⅓" thick.

5. Mix the remaining Splenda with the cardamom and cinnamon in a small bowl.

6. Sprinkle the dough with the Splenda and spice mixture; scatter the raisins and nuts on top.

7. Spray a cookie sheet with nonstick spray.

Swedish Coffee Bread

(continued)

When a Bread Really Is a Meal

Breads like this can be a meal, a snack, or even a dessert. Be creative in how you help your child weave them into her day.

8. Cut the dough in three 6" pieces. Braid the pieces together and place on the cookie sheet. Cover and let rise for 60 minutes.

9. When the dough has doubled in size, heat oven to 350°F.

10. Beat the remaining egg. Brush the dough with egg and bake 25–30 minutes.

YIELDS 1 LOAF;
SERVING SIZE 1 SLICE (12 SLICES PER LOAF)

Calories: 370 | Carbohydrates: 47g | Fat: 17g | Sodium: 230mg | Fiber: 5g

Asian-Flavored Burgers

Miniaturize these tasty snacks to make bite-sized sliders.

INGREDIENTS

1 pound freshly ground chuck or sirloin beef

¼ cup green onions, minced

2 tablespoons Asian ginger dipping sauce

Salt and pepper to taste

1. Combine all ingredients. Divide and form into patties.

2. Prepare your grill or fry pan with nonstick spray. Set on medium-high heat. Grill the burgers to desired level of doneness. Serve hot on Portuguese rolls or with tortilla wraps.

YIELDS 4 SERVINGS; SERVING SIZE 4 OUNCES

Calories: 160 | Carbohydrates: 3g | Fat: 7g | Sodium: 350mg | Fiber: 0g

Greek Lamb-and-Pasta Casserole

This dish has a delightful tang and richness. You can make it in advance to serve the next day or freeze and serve the next week.

INGREDIENTS

1 tablespoon olive oil

1 pound lean ground lamb

1 large sweet onion, chopped

4 cloves garlic, minced

½ cup currants

Salt and freshly ground pepper to taste

½ teaspoon cinnamon

1 teaspoon Splenda

1 teaspoon dried mint or 1 tablespoon fresh mint, chopped

3 cups parboiled orzo

½ cup chicken stock or broth

½ cup toasted pine nuts

1. Preheat the oven to 350°F. Prepare a casserole dish with nonstick cooking spray. Heat the olive oil in a large pan over medium heat. Sauté the meat, onion, and garlic, stirring constantly.

2. Add the currants, salt, pepper, cinnamon, Splenda, and mint.

3. Mix the meat mixture with the orzo and pour into the casserole dish. Stir in the stock or broth. Sprinkle with pine nuts. Bake for 30 minutes.

YIELDS 6 SERVINGS; SERVING SIZE 4 OUNCES

Calories: 420 | Carbohydrates: 25g | Fat: 25g | Sodium: 130mg | Fiber: 2g

Geography Dinners

Why not make each international meal an educational and cultural experience? Find an age-appropriate book about the nation whose cuisine you are sampling and read it with your child that night.

Mexican Shrimp with Chipotles

Serve the shrimp in toasted sugar-free corn tortillas.

INGREDIENTS

1 tablespoon olive oil

½ cup chopped sweet onion

3 cloves garlic, minced

4 ripe tomatoes, diced

2 chipotle peppers, finely chopped

Salt and freshly ground black pepper to taste

1 teaspoon red pepper flakes

1 pound shrimp

1 tablespoon minced cilantro or parsley

1. Heat the oil in a large sauté pan over medium heat. Sauté the onion and garlic.

2. Stir in the tomatoes, chipotle peppers, salt, black pepper, and red pepper flakes. Cook until slightly thickened. Add the shrimp; cook for about 4 minutes, flipping shrimp to cook thoroughly. Garnish with cilantro or parsley if desired. Serve immediately.

YIELDS 4 SERVINGS; SERVING SIZE 4 OUNCES

Calories: 200 | Carbohydrates: 11g | Fat: 6g | Sodium: 180mg | Fiber: 3g

Mexican Tomato Salad

Queso blanco (or queso fresco) is a white Mexican cheese, slightly salty, with a texture like Farmer's cheese.

INGREDIENTS

2 large, round ripe tomatoes, sliced ¼" thick

1 red onion, thinly sliced

2 serrano or jalapeño chilies, thinly sliced

1 tablespoon chopped cilantro leaves

¼ cup queso blanco, crumbled

1 teaspoon dried oregano

1 teaspoon minced garlic

1 tablespoon extra-virgin olive oil

1 tablespoon white wine vinegar

Salt and freshly ground black pepper to taste

1. Arrange the sliced tomatoes, red onions, and chilies on a chilled platter. Sprinkle the cilantro and queso blanco over the top.

2. In a small bowl, combine the remaining ingredients. Drizzle this vinaigrette over the salad just before serving.

SERVES 4

Calories: 100 | Carbohydrates: 8g | Fat: 6g | Sodium: 100mg | Fiber: 2g

What Is Jicama?

Jicama is often referred to as the Mexican potato. It is a large bulbous root vegetable with a thin brown skin and white crunchy flesh. It has a sweet, nutty flavor that is good both raw and cooked. Fresh jicama can be added to salads for a satisfying crunchy texture. Jicama contains 3.8g of carbohydrates per ⅓ cup.

French Roasted Duck with Lemon

Meat left over from the duck carcass can be used in a crepe filling or as a duck salad on a bed of greens.

INGREDIENTS

3 lemons

4½-pound ready-to-cook duck

Salt

Freshly ground black pepper

3 tablespoons butter, divided

2 teaspoons sugar

2 tablespoons white wine vinegar

1 (16-ounce) can chicken stock

3 tablespoons beef broth

1. Preheat oven to 375°F. Cut the rind from 2 of the lemons as thinly as possible. (A vegetable peeler works well.) Juice 1 of the lemons and set aside the juice. Separate the other lemon into segments and set aside. Cut the rind into narrow strips and cook in boiling water for 5 minutes. Rinse with cold water and pat dry.

2. Season inside of the duck with salt and pepper. Place half of the lemon rind and half the butter inside. Truss the duck by tying the legs together with a piece of white butcher's twine. Place the duck on a rack in a roasting pan just large enough to hold the duck without the skin touching the sides. Season the outside of the duck with salt and pepper.

3. Roast the duck, uncovered, for about 1 hour and 15 minutes, or until the leg meat begins to separate from the bone. (Cover the duck with a tent made of aluminum foil after about 45 minutes of cooking if the skin appears to be browning too rapidly.) Baste the duck with its natural juices during the roasting process.

French Roasted Duck with Lemon

(continued)

Duck Salad Sandwiches

All the little bits of meat that fall off the bone or leftovers that are rough-chopped or sliced make for wonderful sandwiches. Combine 1 cup of chopped or shredded meat with 2 or 3 tablespoons of good-quality mayonnaise for the simplest sandwich spread. Jazz it up a bit with 2 table-spoons of any of the following: tapenade, diced sun-dried tomatoes, diced pimiento, arti-choke relish, or finely chopped red onion.

4. Remove duck from the oven. Do not discard the cooking juices from the pan. Let the duck rest for at least 30 minutes before carving, keeping it tented with foil in a warm place.

5. In a medium-size saucepan over medium heat, cook the sugar and vinegar together, stirring often, until a caramel has formed. Add a little chicken stock and stir, scraping the bottom of the saucepan. Add the rest of the stock, the reserved lemon juice, and the remaining lemon rind strips. Add any natural juices remaining from the roasting pan; simmer over medium heat until the sauce is thick enough to coat the back of a spoon. Add the reserved lemon segments and the rest of the butter; simmer for another 5 minutes.

6. To serve, arrange slices of breast meat on a warmed plate and drizzle the sauce over the top. Garnish with slices cut from the remaining lemon.

SERVES 10

Calories: 870 | Carbohydrates: 2g | Fat: 84g | Sodium: 230mg | Fiber: 0g

Chicken Cacciatore

*The vegetables increase the carb count
of this recipe to a moderate level.*

INGREDIENTS

¼ cup olive oil

1 (3½-pound) chicken, cut into 8
   pieces

Salt and freshly ground black
   pepper

2 medium onions, thinly sliced
   into rings

3 cloves garlic, finely chopped

1¼ cups thinly sliced button
   mushrooms

1 small green bell pepper, thinly
   sliced

¼ cup tomato paste

¾ cup chicken broth

16 ounces canned plum tomatoes

½ teaspoon dried rosemary

½ teaspoon dried oregano

Freshly grated Parmesan cheese
   for garnish

1. Heat the olive oil in a large skillet on
   high heat to almost smoking.

2. Season the chicken with salt and
   pepper; fry it, skin-side down, for 5
   minutes, or until lightly browned.
   Turn over and brown the other side.
   Remove the chicken pieces with a
   slotted spoon and set aside.

3. Reduce heat to medium. Add the
   onions to the pan; cook 5 minutes;
   add the garlic, mushrooms, and
   green pepper. Cook for another 3–4
   minutes, or until the onions are
   golden, stirring frequently.

4. Mix in the tomato paste and chicken
   broth; cook for 1–2 minutes, then
   add the tomatoes, breaking them
   down with a wooden spoon. Sprinkle in the rosemary and oregano.
   Return the chicken to the pan. Season with salt and pepper, cover, and
   simmer for 30 minutes, stirring
   occasionally.

5. Check the chicken to ensure it is
   cooked and tender. If it is still resis-
   tant when pierced with a fork, cover

Chicken Cacciatore

(continued)

Garlic Done Easy

Most supermarket produce sections carry fresh garlic already cleaned, in jars or plastic containers. Older garlic cloves will appear wrinkled and spotted and are bitter. Make sure the cloves have an unblemished, even, ivory color, which indicates freshness.

and cook for another 10 minutes. The leg meat should easily pull away from the bone.

6. Using a slotted spoon, transfer the chicken pieces to a serving plate; keep warm. If the sauce appears too liquid, allow it to lightly boil, uncovered, for 5 minutes to slightly thicken.

7. Season to taste, then pour sauce over the chicken. Serve immediately. Garnish with freshly grated Parmesan cheese.

SERVES 4

Calories: 910 | Carbohydrates: 18g | Fat: 51g | Sodium: 400mg | Fiber: 4g

Fusion Lo Mein

Combining this tropical-flavored vegetable stir-fry with cooked pasta creates a deliciously different lo mein. At over 1 cup per serving, it's a large side dish that's low enough in calories to accompany a meat course.

INGREDIENTS

2 tablespoons rice vinegar

2 tablespoons thawed pineapple-orange juice concentrate

2 teaspoons minced shallots

2 teaspoons lemon juice

1 teaspoon cornstarch

1 teaspoon Worcestershire sauce

1 teaspoon honey

2 cloves garlic, minced

1 teaspoon olive oil

¾ cup chopped green onions

1 cup diagonally sliced (¼"-thick) carrots

1 cup julienned yellow bell pepper

1 cup julienned red bell pepper

3 cups small broccoli florets

1 cup fresh bean sprouts

1½ cups cooked pasta

1. In a food processor or blender, combine the vinegar, juice concentrate, shallots, lemon juice, cornstarch, Worcestershire, honey, and garlic; process until smooth.

2. Heat a wok or large nonstick skillet coated with cooking spray over medium-high heat until hot, then add the olive oil. Add the onions; stir-fry for 1 minute. Add the carrots, bell peppers, and broccoli; stir-fry for another minute. Cover the pan and cook for 2 more minutes. Add the vinegar mixture and the sprouts. Bring the mixture to a boil and cook, uncovered, for 30 seconds, stirring constantly. Add the cooked pasta and toss to mix.

SERVES 6

Calories: 140 | Carbohydrates: 27g | Fat: 2g | Sodium: 45mg | Fiber: 3g

Guiltless Pasta

Pasta like lo mein need not be removed from your family list. This homemade recipe keeps the carbs within reason but still gives that exotic meal feel.

Cheese Fondue
with Dipping Vegetables

This is an interactive appetizer or main course that's almost as much about the event of the meal as it is about the food itself.

INGREDIENTS

1 clove garlic, mashed

1 cup chicken broth

1 pound imported Swiss cheese, such as Jarlsberg, coarsely grated

¼ teaspoon ground nutmeg

Freshly ground pepper to taste

Salt to taste

2 egg yolks, beaten

2 tablespoons gluten-free flour, such as potato flour

½ cup cream

1 broccoli crown, blanched in boiling water for 2 minutes, cooled and cut in pieces

2 sweet red peppers, cored, seeded, and cut into chunks

½ pound sugar snap peas, rinsed

2 zucchini and/or 12 very thin asparagus tips, cut up

* Optional: 1 loaf gluten-free French-style bread, cubed and toasted

1. In a large pot or chafing dish over a burner, heat the garlic in the broth.

2. Stir in the cheese, nutmeg, pepper, and salt. Mix slowly over low flame.

3. In a separate bowl, whisk together the egg yolks, flour, and cream. Stir into the cheese mixture.

4. When the cheese mixture has melted, enjoy by spearing veggies or bread on a long-handled fork and dipping into the cheese mixture. If the cheese gets too thick, add a bit more warm broth.

SERVES 14

Calories: 200 | Carbohydrates: 10g | Fat: 12g | Sodium: 170mg | Fiber: 2g

Zabaglione

This is an interactive dessert. If it's made in a chafing dish, guests can take turns whisking until the mixture foams up in a stunning show. You can serve this dish over sliced fruit such as strawberries, raspberries, or blueberries.

INGREDIENTS

6 egg yolks

½ cup sugar substitute

⅔ cup Marsala wine

The Art of Double Boiling

To make a double boiler, simmer about 1" of water in a deep saucepan. Set a glass or metal bowl on the top of the saucepan. Take care that the simmering water does not touch the bottom of the bowl, or you will scramble the eggs!

1. Set up the chafing dish but don't light the sterno or oil. Beat the egg yolks and sugar substitute together with an electric mixer until a very pale, lemon yellow.

2. Whisk in the wine. Light the burner and place a pan of warm water in the base. Add egg mixture to the brazier pan.

3. Slowly heat the mixture, whisking constantly until it suddenly foams up and thickens slightly. Don't overcook, or you'll have Marsala-flavored scrambled eggs!

SERVES 6

Calories: 100 | Carbohydrates: 6g | Fat: 4.5g | Sodium: 10mg | Fiber: 0g

Tomatillo Salsa

Green salsa (salsa verde) is usually made with roasted bell peppers.
This version, made with tomatillos, is tangy and spicy.

INGREDIENTS

¾ pound tomatillos, husked

1 jalapeño pepper

1 habanero pepper

½ cup water

1 tablespoon olive oil

4 cloves garlic, minced

1 large onion, chopped

½ teaspoon salt

¼ teaspoon pepper

½ cup chopped cilantro

¼ cup chopped flat-leaf parsley

1. Rinse tomatillos and chop coarsely. Combine in a saucepan with jalapeño and habanero peppers and water; bring to a boil. Reduce heat and simmer, stirring frequently, 5 minutes. Remove from heat, drain, and set aside.

2. In medium skillet, heat olive oil over medium heat. Add garlic and onion; cook and stir until crisp-tender, about 5–6 minutes. Remove from heat.

3. In blender or food processor, combine tomatillo mixture, onion mixture, and remaining ingredients. Blend or process until desired consistency. Cover and chill 2–3 hours to blend flavors.

YIELDS 2 CUPS; SERVING SIZE ¼ CUP

Calories: 40 | Carbohydrates: 5g | Fat: 2g | Sodium: 150mg | Fiber: 1g

What Are Tomatillos?

Tomatillos are small green fruits with a papery covering. Remove the covering and rinse before using. They are not green tomatoes; in fact, they are a type of berry, related to the gooseberry. They can be eaten raw or cooked, although cooking does make them a bit less tart and crunchy.

CHAPTER 13

Decadent Diabetes Desserts

Peanut Butter Pleaser

Easy to make and so yummy, this recipe is one your kids
will beg to not just eat, but create.

INGREDIENTS

1 tablespoon plus 1 teaspoon
    unsalted, smooth peanut
    butter

1 teaspoon vanilla extract

⅞ cup Mock Whipped Cream (see
    page 214)

In a bowl, fold the peanut butter and
vanilla into the Mock Whipped Cream
until well blended. Chill until ready to
serve.

SERVES 4

Calories: 100 | Carbohydrates: 8g | Fat: 2.5g |
Sodium: 75mg | Fiber: 0g

Orange Carrot Cake GF

*This delicious cake has a nice zing with the addition
of a little lemon juice and the grated orange rind.
The gingerroot adds an appealing sophistication.*

INGREDIENTS

4 eggs, separated

½ cup brown sugar

1½ cups grated carrots

1 tablespoon lemon juice

Grated rind of ½ fresh orange

½ cup corn flour

1" fresh gingerroot, peeled and
   minced

1½ teaspoons baking soda

½ teaspoon salt

Treats Done Right Are Great!

Kids love dessert, and it's
important you show your child
with diabetes that like any
child, he can enjoy delicious
desserts. Just be sure to point
out to him that all children—
with or without diabetes—
should enjoy treats in
moderation.

1. Liberally butter a springform pan
   and preheat oven to 325°F. Beat the
   egg whites until stiff and set aside.

2. Beat the egg yolks, sugar, and carrots together. Add lemon juice;
   orange rind, and corn flour. When
   smooth, add the gingerroot, baking
   soda, and salt. Gently fold in the
   egg whites.

3. Pour the cake batter into the springform pan; bake for 1 hour. Test by
   plunging a toothpick into the center
   of the cake—if the pick comes out
   clean, the cake is done.

SERVES 8–10

Calories: 100 | Carbohydrates: 17g | Fat: 2g |
Sodium: 350mg | Fiber: 1g

Banana Brownies

These actually taste a lot richer than they are!
They satisfy your sweet tooth and make use of your overripe bananas.

INGREDIENTS

2 mashed bananas

¾ cup Splenda

½ cup buttery spread

1 egg

¾ cup hot water

6 ounces unsweetened chocolate, melted

2 cups all purpose flour

½ teaspoon salt

1 teaspoon ground cinnamon

1. Preheat oven to 300°F. Prepare a 13" × 9" baking pan with nonstick spray. In a large mixing bowl, beat the bananas, Splenda, buttery spread, egg, water, and chocolate together.

2. Add the flour, salt, and cinnamon to the chocolate mixture. Blend well. Pour into the pan.

3. Bake the brownies for 45 minutes, or until toothpick inserted in center comes out clean.

YIELDS 36 BROWNIES;
SERVING SIZE 1 BROWNIE

Calories: 80 | Carbohydrates: 9g | Fat: 5g |
Sodium: 55mg | Fiber: 1g

Chocolate Fluff

This is a super-easy version of Bavarian cream that is quite easy to make. The addition of orange juice contributes a great deal to the flavor.

INGREDIENTS

3 ounces unsweetened baking chocolate

2 tablespoons Splenda

¼ ounce unflavored gelatin

2 ounces cold water

6 ounces orange juice

4 egg whites

½ cup whipping cream

Become an Egg White Whipping Master

When you whip egg whites, they will not get stiff unless your bowl and beaters or whisk are immaculately clean. If there is a touch of fat or grease on them, your eggs will not puff up. If you are beating both egg whites and whipping cream, do the eggs first. Then rinse the beaters and whip the cream.

1. Melt the chocolate and set aside. Place the Splenda, gelatin, and water in a blender. Let it expand a bit. Meanwhile, heat the orange juice, but don't boil it.

2. Add the hot orange juice to the Splenda and gelatin mixture. Blend until the gelatin has dissolved. Blend in the chocolate. Let cool to room temperature.

3. Beat the egg whites until they are stiff; set aside. Whip the cream. Pour the chocolate mixture into a large bowl.

4. Gently fold the egg whites into the chocolate mixture; fold in the whipped cream.

5. Chill, mixing occasionally, bringing the chocolate up from the bottom of the bowl. Serve in wine glasses.

YIELDS 8 SERVINGS; SERVING SIZE 1 CUP

Calories: 130 | Carbohydrates: 7g | Fat: 11g | Sodium: 330mg | Fiber: 2g

Chocolate Meringue Cookies

You can make petite cookies by using a teaspoon measure of batter instead of a tablespoon.

INGREDIENTS

3 large eggs, separated

⅛ teaspoon cream of tartar

¾ cup granulated sugar

3 tablespoons unsweetened cocoa powder, plus extra for garnish

Getting Cheesy with It

Tradition dictates that dessert, or the ending course of a formal meal, include something sweet and carbohydrate heavy. Consider ending the meal in the European style, by serving a sophisticated cheese course with a very simple dessert, such as a small platter of petite cookies for those desiring something sweet.

1. Preheat the oven to 375°F. Cover 2 baking sheets with parchment paper.

2. Place the egg whites and cream of tartar in a medium-size bowl or the bowl of an electric mixer; mix on medium-high speed until soft peaks form. Gradually beat in the granulated sugar (1 tablespoon at a time) until the whites are stiff and shiny.

3. Sift the cocoa over the egg whites; gently fold in until just blended. Drop tablespoons of the batter 1" apart on the prepared baking sheets. Bake 30–35 minutes, until the cookies are dry. Carefully peel the cookies from the paper and cool on a wire rack. When cool, sprinkle the cookies with a little more cocoa powder. Store, covered, at room temperature.

SERVES 12

Calories: 70 | Carbohydrates: 13g | Fat: 1.5g | Sodium: 20mg | Fiber: 0g

Individual Sponge Cakes

Don't let the whole eggs in this recipe scare you away. They provide the only fat in the recipe. That's right! It doesn't call for any oil or butter. Try these as shortcakes with unsweetened fruit and some whipped topping.

INGREDIENTS

1 cup flour

½ teaspoon salt

1 teaspoon baking powder

3 eggs

¾ cup granulated sugar

1 tablespoon lemon juice

½ teaspoon lemon zest (optional)

6 tablespoons hot milk

Can I Jazz Up these Cakes?

Yes! Use a pastry bag to pump some nonfat whipped topping or low-sugar jelly (or a mixture of the two) into the center of the Individual Sponge Cakes, and you have a healthier homemade snack cake alternative.

1. Preheat oven to 350°F. Mix together the flour, salt, and baking powder. Set aside. In a food processor or mixing bowl, beat the eggs until fluffy and lemon colored. Add the sugar, lemon juice, and, if using, the lemon zest. Add the flour mixture; process only enough to blend. Add the hot milk; process until blended.

2. Pour into a 12-section muffin pan treated with nonstick spray. (Also works well as 24 mini muffins.) If lining the muffin pan, use foil liners. Bake for 15 minutes, or until a toothpick inserted in the center of a cupcake comes out clean. The cakes will be golden brown and firm to the touch. Move the cupcakes to a rack to cool.

**YIELDS 12 CUPCAKES;
SERVING SIZE 1 CUPCAKE**

Calories: 110 | Carbohydrates: 21g | Fat: 1.5g | Sodium: 160mg | Fiber: 0g

Mock Whipped Cream

There is some fat in this recipe, but the use of vegetable oil reduces the saturated fat and cholesterol amounts considerably compared to making whipped cream using real cream.

INGREDIENTS

1 envelope unflavored gelatine

¼ cup cold water

½ cup hot water

2 tablespoons almond oil

1 teaspoon vanilla

3 tablespoons powdered sugar

1 cup ice water

1¼ cups nonfat milk powder

1. Allow the gelatin to soften in the cold water, then pour the mixture into a blender. Add the hot water; blend for 2 minutes, until the gelatin is dissolved.

2. While continuing to blend the mixture, gradually add the almond oil, vanilla, and powdered sugar. Chill in the freezer for 15 minutes, or until the mixture is cool but hasn't yet begun to set.

3. Using a hand mixer or whisk, add the ice water and nonfat milk powder to a chilled bowl; beat until peaks start to form. Add the gelatin mixture to the whipped milk; continue to whip until stiffer peaks begin to form. This whipped topping will keep several days in the refrigerator. Whip again to reintroduce more air into the topping before serving.

**YIELDS 3½ CUPS;
SERVING SIZE 2 TABLESPOONS**

Calories: 35 | Carbohydrates: 4g | Fat: 1g | Sodium: 30mg | Fiber: 0g

Watermelon-Lime Sorbet

If you don't have an ice cream maker,
freeze this in your freezer.

INGREDIENTS

2 cups sweet watermelon, seeds
removed

2 tablespoons Splenda

Juice of 1 lime

½ teaspoon salt

1. Combine the melon, Splenda, lime juice, and salt in a food processor.

2. Following the directions on an ice cream maker, freeze the sorbet. If you don't have an ice cream maker, freeze the sorbet in a baking dish in your freezer, breaking it up with a fork every 30 minutes until thoroughly frozen.

YIELDS 6 SERVINGS; SERVING SIZE ½ CUP

Calories: 20 | Carbohydrates: 5g | Fat: 0g |
Sodium: 190mg | Fiber: 0g

Chocolate Cheesecake Mousse

"Mmmmm chocolate" is what you'll hear when serving this treat.

INGREDIENTS

1 tablespoon semisweet chocolate chips

¾ cups Mock Whipped Cream, divided (see page 214)

1 ounce cream cheese

1½ teaspoon cocoa

1 teaspoon vanilla

1. Put the chocolate chips and 1 tablespoon of the Mock Whipped Cream in a microwave-safe bowl; microwave on high for 15 seconds.

2. Add the cream cheese to the bowl; microwave on high for another 15 seconds. Whip the mixture until it is well blended and the chocolate chips are melted.

3. Stir in the cocoa and vanilla. Fold in the remaining Mock Whipped Cream. Chill until ready to serve.

SERVES 4

Calories: 90 | Carbohydrates: 8g | Fat: 3.5 | Sodium: 65mg | Fiber: 0g

Frosted Blueberries with Peach Ice

This is an icy treat on a hot day, and great at night, too!

INGREDIENTS

1 cup fresh blueberries

1 tablespoon powdered sugar

4 fresh peaches, blanched, halved, pitted, and skins removed

Juice of ½ lemon

½ cup sugar substitute

1½ cups water

1. Cover a baking sheet with aluminum foil. Rinse blueberries. While the berries are still damp, place them on the baking sheet. Freeze for 2 hours; then sprinkle the berries with powdered sugar, roll to coat, cover with plastic wrap, and return the sheet to the freezer.

2. Place the peaches, lemon juice, sugar substitute, and water in the blender. Purée until very smooth.

3. Pour the peach mixture into an ice cube tray and freeze for 2 hours. If you don't have an ice cube tray, use a small, medium-sided pan and break up completely. Remove and break up with a fork. Continue to freeze until you have a very grainy, icy mixture.

4. Fold the peach slush and frozen blueberries together. Serve in goblets.

SERVES 4

Calories: 100 | Carbohydrates: 26g | Fat: 0.5g | Sodium: 0mg | Fiber: 3g

Chocolate Fudge

*The quality of the chocolate is key;
purchase quality imported chocolate if available.*

INGREDIENTS

1 cup heavy cream

8 ounces unsweetened chocolate, chopped

1¾ cups sugar substitute, granular style

2 tablespoons unsalted butter

1 tablespoon vanilla extract

1. Line a baking sheet with waxed paper or parchment paper. Spray with nonstick coating.

2. Place a medium-size saucepan over medium heat; add the cream. Bring to a boil, add the chocolate, and stir until completely melted. Remove the pan from the heat and add the sugar substitute, butter, and vanilla extract. Mix until smooth and thoroughly combined.

3. Transfer mixture to the prepared baking sheet. Spread evenly over the entire sheet. Refrigerate until cool and stiff, about 2 hours. To serve, cut the fudge into squares.

SERVES 40

Calories: 60 | Carbohydrates: 3g | Fat: 6g | Sodium: 0mg | Fiber: <1g

Rhubarb and Strawberry Cream

The season for fresh rhubarb is short—peak growing periods are April through June. Think about helping your child grown her own!

INGREDIENTS

4 cups diced rhubarb

11 packets sugar substitute

Pinch of salt

1 pint strawberries, cut into small pieces, plus extra for garnish

1 pint heavy cream

A Simple Finish When Berries Are in Season

Combine ⅓ cup sliced strawberries (3.5g carbohydrate), 1 teaspoon honey (5.8g carbohydrate), and ¼ cup vanilla yogurt (2.6g carbohydrate) for an easy and delicious treat.

1. Put the diced rhubarb into a medium-size saucepan; stew it gently, uncovered. You may need to add a tablespoon of water. Add 9 packets of sugar substitute and salt. Cook until the rhubarb is very tender and can be mashed easily with a fork. Add additional water as needed, tablespoon by tablespoon, to prevent the rhubarb from scorching. Add the strawberries; cook just until combined with the rhubarb mixture, about 4 minutes. Cool the mixture in the refrigerator for about 1 hour.

2. Whip the cream until stiff peaks have formed. Mix in the remaining 2 packets of sugar substitute. Using a rubber spatula, gently fold the whipped cream into the rhubarb mixture. Spoon the mousse into individual ramekins or small serving dishes, cover with plastic wrap, and chill thoroughly before serving. Serve with a garnish of fresh strawberries.

SERVES 8

Calories: 240 | Carbohydrates: 9g | Fat: 22g | Sodium: 45mg | Fiber: 2g

No-Crust Cheesecake

You can vary the flavor by substituting different extracts for the citrus extracts, but always add the vanilla extract.

INGREDIENTS

1 tablespoon butter, for greasing pan

2 pounds cream cheese, at room temperature

1 cup sugar substitute

4 large eggs, at room temperature

¼ teaspoon orange extract

¼ teaspoon lemon extract

2 tablespoons heavy cream

1 teaspoon pure vanilla extract

1. Preheat oven to 350°F. Butter the bottom and sides of a 9" springform pan and set aside.

2. Using an electric mixer, beat the cream cheese on medium speed until it's very smooth. Slowly beat in the sugar substitute, 1 tablespoon at a time. Then add the eggs 1 at a time, beating well after each addition. Add the remaining ingredients, scrape down the bowl, and stir to combine.

3. Pour the cheesecake batter into the prepared springform pan and smooth the top with a rubber spatula. Bake for 10 minutes. Turn down the heat to 275°F and bake for approximately 1 hour, or until the edges are lightly brown (the cheesecake may be cracked on top). Turn off the oven.

4. Remove the cheesecake from the oven, run a thin-bladed knife around the edge of the pan, and return the pan to the oven to cool slowly. Don't be concerned if the center of the

No-Crust Cheesecake

(continued)

Cheesecake Cracking

Sometimes cheesecakes crack while as they cool. You can prevent this by baking them in a warm water bath. Wrap the springform pan in foil and place it in a larger pan. Add hot water to come 1" up the side of the springform pan. Bake as directed. If the top still cracks, try adding a thin layer of Mock Whipped Cream (page 214) to hide any faults!

cheesecake still looks a little under-cooked; it will firm up in the oven as it slowly cools.

5. Cover the cooled cheesecake with the plastic wrap and refrigerate overnight, or up to 3 days. To serve, run a knife around the edges again and remove the sides of the spring-form pan.

SERVES 12

Calories: 310 | Carbohydrates: 4g | Fat: 30g | Sodium: 250mg | Fiber: 0g

Orange Mousse with Blueberries

*The sharply orange flavor of this mousse is counterbalanced
with the sweetness of the blueberries.
You can also substitute lemon zest for the orange zest.*

INGREDIENTS

½ ounce unflavored gelatin

¼ cup cold orange juice

1½ cups orange juice, heated

2 tablespoons finely zested
orange peel

½ teaspoon salt

½ cup Splenda

3 egg whites

½ cup whipping cream

1 pint blueberries

Thinly sliced orange for garnish

1. Place the gelatin and cold orange juice in a blender. Let the gelatin soften for about 5 minutes. Add the hot orange juice, zest, salt, and Splenda. Blend until smooth.

2. Pour the orange mixture in a large bowl. Set aside.

3. Beat the egg whites until they are stiff. Rinse the beaters and beat the cream.

4. Gently fold the egg whites and then the cream into the orange mixture. Refrigerate and stir occasionally.

5. Just before serving, mix in the blueberries. Garnish with orange slices.

YIELDS 8 SERVINGS; SERVING SIZE ½ CUP

Calories: 120 | Carbohydrates: 13g | Fat: 6g |
Sodium: 180mg | Fiber: 1g

Fresh Fruit Sauce

*Making fresh fruit sauces is a snap. They are a great alternative
to sugary sauces and toppings you find in the supermarket.*

INGREDIENTS

1 pint of raspberries, strawberries,
or blueberries, hulled

2 tablespoons Splenda, or to taste

1. Put berries and Splenda into a
   blender. Blend until smooth.

2. Put through a sieve if grainy. Pour
   into a jar and refrigerate. Use over
   any dessert that needs a fruit sauce.

YIELDS 1 PINT; SERVING SIZE 2 TABLESPOONS

Calories: 10 for raspberries and blueberries; 5 for
strawberries | Carbohydrates: 2g for raspberries
and strawberries; 3g for blueberries | Fat: 0g |
Sodium: 0mg | Fiber: <1g

Peach Parfait

Parfait means "perfect" in French. Letting kids build their own perfect dessert makes them feel like it's really something special. This recipe lends itself well to that process.

INGREDIENTS

4 cups water

4 ripe peaches

4 teaspoons lemon juice

½ cup whipping cream

1 teaspoon Splenda

¼ cup Fresh Fruit Sauce (use raspberries) (page 223)

2 teaspoons slivered almonds, toasted

1. Bring 4 cups of water to a boil in a two-quart saucepan over medium heat. Add the peaches; cook for 3–4 minutes, or until skin begins to look dull and puffed. Drain the water. Slip the skins off, then slice the peaches into a bowl.

2. Sprinkle the peaches with lemon juice. Whip the cream with the Splenda; set aside.

3. Divide the peaches among four wine glasses. Add a teaspoon of fresh raspberry sauce to each glass. Repeat with a second layer of each.

4. Top each parfait with whipped cream and sprinkle the top with almonds. Serve chilled.

YIELDS 4 SERVINGS; SERVING SIZE ½ CUP

Calories: 175 | Carbohydrates: 18g | Fat: 12g | Sodium: 10mg | Fiber: 2g

Raspberry Granité

Nothing tastes fresher than the pure fruit ice in this recipe.

INGREDIENTS

1 quart raspberries

1 cup water

4 packets sugar substitute

1 tablespoon lemon juice

Pinch of salt

1. Bring all ingredients to a boil in a medium saucepan.

2. Reduce heat and simmer, covered, for 10 minutes, or until the sugar substitute melts.

3. Force the mixture through a sieve and freeze in a shallow pan or ice cube tray, breaking up with a fork occasionally. Continue to freeze and break apart the granité until you have a very grainy, icy mixture.

SERVES 4

Calories: 70 | Carbohydrates: 16g | Fat: 1g | Sodium: 40mg | Fiber: 1g

Flourless Chocolate Cake

Use the best-quality gluten-free chocolate you can find for this rich cake.
Callebaut is an excellent brand.

INGREDIENTS

1 tablespoon coconut oil

2 teaspoons gluten-free cocoa powder

6 (1-ounce) squares gluten-free bittersweet chocolate, chopped

2 (1-ounce) squares gluten-free semisweet chocolate, chopped

⅓ cup coconut oil

3 tablespoons vegetable oil

¾ cup sugar

¼ teaspoon salt

¼ cup brown sugar

¼ cup gluten-free cocoa powder

1 teaspoon gluten-free vanilla

4 eggs

5 (1-ounce) squares gluten-free semisweet chocolate, chopped

1. Preheat oven to 300°F.

2. Grease a 10" springform pan with 1 tablespoon coconut oil and dust with 2 teaspoons cocoa powder; set aside.

3. In heavy saucepan, combine both chopped chocolates, coconut oil, vegetable oil, sugar, salt, and brown sugar over low heat. Cook and stir until chocolate and coconut oil melt and sugar dissolves, stirring frequently. Pour into large bowl.

4. Add cocoa powder and vanilla; beat for 1 minute. Then add eggs, one at a time, beating well after each addition.

5. Pour batter into prepared pan. Bake 50–60 minutes, or until cake jiggles just slightly in the center when pushed.

6. Let cool on wire rack; chill overnight in the refrigerator before removing pan.

Flourless Chocolate Cake

(continued)

Melting Chocolate

There are a few rules to follow when melting chocolate. Make sure that you don't allow even a drop of water to come into contact with the chocolate; it will make the chocolate seize and turn grainy. Use low heat, and stir very frequently, if not constantly, so it doesn't burn.

7. Unmold cake and place on serving plate.

8. In microwave-safe bowl, melt 5 ounces semisweet chocolate on 50 percent power 2–3 minutes; stir until smooth.

9. Spoon over the cake and smooth with offset spatula. Let stand until firm. Cut into very small pieces to serve.

SERVES 16

Calories: 250 | Carbohydrates: 27g | Fat: 18g | Sodium: 55mg | Fiber: 2g

Banana-Orange Cupcakes

A yummy cupcake with less than 30g of carbs?
Now that's sweet.

INGREDIENTS

1½ cups all-purpose flour

½ cup whole-wheat flour

1½ teaspoons baking powder

½ teaspoon baking soda

½ teaspoon salt

¼ cup olive or vegetable oil

1 ripe banana, mashed

¾ cup rice milk

½ cup gluten-free orange juice

¼ cup honey

2 teaspoons gluten-free vanilla

2 teaspoons grated orange zest

1 cup gluten-free powdered sugar

2 tablespoons orange juice

Bananas in Baking

Make sure that the bananas you use in baking are very ripe. The skins should be yellow, with no green color at all, and dotted with black. Bananas are a good substitute for eggs in most baking recipes, since they add moisture and a bit of structure to the batter. Should you have a lot of ripe bananas on hand, they freeze very well, whole or mashed.

1. Preheat oven to 350°F. In large bowl, combine flours, baking powder, baking soda, and salt; mix well with wire whisk.

2. In medium bowl, combine oil, banana, and rice milk; mash together using a potato masher. Stir in ½ cup orange juice, honey, vanilla, and orange zest; mix well.

3. Add banana mixture all at once to the dry ingredients; mix until combined. Stir 1 minute.

4. Fill cups (use paper liners if you like or lightly grease if not) ¾ full. Bake 18–23 minutes, or until cupcakes are set and light golden brown. Let cool on wire rack 10 minutes.

5. In small bowl, combine powdered sugar and 2 tablespoons orange juice; mix well. Drizzle over warm cupcakes. Let cool completely.

YIELDS 18 CUPCAKES

Calories: 130 | Carbohydrates: 24g | Fat: 3.5g | Sodium: 140mg | Fiber: <1g

CHAPTER 14

Takeout Made In

Chimichangas

*Chimichangas are usually deep-fried,
but this baked version is easier, and better for your family, too.*

INGREDIENTS

1 pound spicy ground gluten-free pork sausage

1 onion, chopped

3 cloves garlic, minced

1 jalapeño pepper, minced

1 green bell pepper, chopped

1 (15-ounce) can refried beans

1 (6-ounce) can gluten-free tomato paste

1 tablespoon chili powder

¼ teaspoon salt

¼ teaspoon white pepper

12 (6") corn tortillas

1½ cups shredded dairy-free, vegan Monterey jack cheese, divided in 8 parts

2 tablespoons vegetable oil

Salsa

Avocado

1. Preheat oven to 375°F. In large saucepan, cook sausage with onion and garlic, stirring to break up meat. Drain well. Return pan to heat. Add jalapeño and green bell pepper; cook and stir 3 minutes.

2. Add refried beans, tomato paste, chili powder, salt, and pepper; mix well. Bring to a simmer; simmer, stirring frequently, 10 minutes.

3. Arrange tortillas on work surface. Place about ¼ cup sausage mixture on each, then top with cheese, using ⅓ of the cheese for each. Roll up and place seam-side down on cookie sheet. Repeat with remaining tortillas, sausage filling, and cheese.

4. Brush Chimichangas with oil; bake 25–35 minutes, or until tortillas are crisp and cheese is melted. Serve immediately with salsa and avocado.

SERVES 8

Calories: 460 | Carbohydrates: 38g | Fat: 23g | Sodium: 1470mg | Fiber: 7g

At Home "Happy Meal"

Kids will tell you part of the fun of takeout food is the setup. Consider adding a surprise toy with your child's homemade "takeout" meal, and serve in a fun container or on a fun plate.

Sausage and Peppers with Melted Mozzarella Cheese

This classic Italian combination is usually served as a sub or hero. Try it on thinly sliced whole-wheat bread and use less sausage and peppers.

INGREDIENTS

¼ pound Italian sausage link, cut in 8 pieces

½ cup thinly sliced sweet white onions

4 thin slices whole-wheat or sourdough bread

4 slices red roasted peppers (from a jar is fine)

4 thin slices mozzarella cheese

2 teaspoons Italian dressing

½ cup shredded Napa cabbage or romaine lettuce

You can also substitute vegetarian sausage for regular sausage and use low-fat cheese.

1. Fry sausage pieces in a nonstick pan over low heat. When brown, drain on paper towels.

2. Add the onions; sizzle over low heat until wilted. Reserve.

3. Toast the bread. Place the sausage slices on 2 pieces of toast. Arrange the onions, peppers, and cheese on top of the sausage.

4. Run under a hot broiler until the cheese melts. Drizzle with dressing. Pile with shredded cabbage or lettuce for crunch.

MAKES 2 SANDWICHES

Calories: 580 | Carbohydrates: 41g | Fat: 35g | Sodium: 1080mg | Fiber: 5g

"Hero" Meals

Subs don't have to be unhealthy. As this recipe shows, you can choose wholesome ingredients and make a sub seem just as special and take-out-ish for kids. Just choose whole-wheat or multi-grain rolls and smart recipes for fillings.

Taco Salad

This is a great way to get kids to eat spinach!

INGREDIENTS

16 taco chips

1 cup grated Cheddar or Monterey jack cheese

1 (10-ounce) bag baby spinach, shredded (or more if you desire)

2 sweet red roasted peppers, chopped

1 sweet onion, chopped

1 cup of your favorite salsa

½ cup sour cream

You can also substitute low-fat sour cream for regular sour cream

1. Arrange the taco chips on 4 broiler-proof serving plates. Sprinkle with cheese; place under broiler until the cheese melts.

2. Top taco chips with spinach, peppers, and onion. Serve with salsa and sour cream on the side.

SERVES 4

Calories: 290 | Carbohydrates: 26g | Fat: 17g | Sodium: 730mg | Fiber: 6g

Kid's Meal from Start to Finish

Food seems to magically taste great when kids take an active role in the preparation. A simple meal like this one can involve your child from the start. Let them make the shopping list, help with the shopping, and then prepare the food. Healthy *and* educational!

Crispy Potato-Crusted Chicken

When you use this crust on your baked chicken, you'll find it's really crispy and crunchy. Don't add salt, as potato chips are already salty.

INGREDIENTS

12 ounces potato chips

4 boneless, skinless chicken breasts

⅔ cup sour cream

1 teaspoon freshly ground black pepper

2 tablespoons snipped fresh chives

1 teaspoon dried thyme

Alternatives to Bread Crumbs

Try using your food processor to make crumbs of such goodies as cornbread, potato chips, or popcorn. Check various rice cereals such as puffed rice and rice crisps to make sure they are gluten free, then put them in your food processor to make crumbs. Store the crumbs in resealable plastic bags in the refrigerator.

1. In a food processor, chop up potato chips until you have 1 cup of crumbs.

2. Rinse the chicken, dry on paper towels, and lay it in a baking dish that you have prepared with nonstick spray.

3. Preheat the oven to 350°F. Spread the chicken with sour cream. Sprinkle with the potato-chip crumbs mixed with the pepper, chives and thyme; bake for 25 minutes, or until brown and crispy.

SERVES 4

Calories: 610 | Carbohydrates: 63g | Fat: 25g | Sodium: 880mg | Fiber: 4g

Texas Burgers

You can make these burgers as spicy or as mild as you like. Just make sure you use sugar-free chili sauce or you'll sweeten them up much too much.

INGREDIENTS

1 pound ground sirloin

Salt and pepper to taste

1 teaspoon garlic powder

1 tablespoon chili powder

½ cup red onion, minced

2 tablespoons sugar-free chili sauce

4 corn tortillas

1. Mix all of the ingredients together. Form into patties.

2. Grill over medium-high flame or under the broiler to desired state of doneness.

3. Serve each burger on a grilled corn tortilla.

YIELDS 4 SERVINGS; SERVING SIZE 4 OUNCES

Calories: 210 | Carbohydrates: 17g | Fat: 6g | Sodium: 190mg | Fiber: 3g

Crispy Sesame Chicken Tenders

This gives you loads of flavor for very few calories. If you and your family are addressing problems of weight, serve this as a snack. High protein, very low fat, and no sugar!

INGREDIENTS

6 chicken tenders (totaling 1 pound)

¼ cup soy sauce

Juice of ½ lime

1 teaspoon Splenda

¼ teaspoon cayenne pepper

½ cup white sesame seeds

1. Cut the tenders in bite-sized pieces. Mix the next four ingredients in a resealable plastic bag. Add the tenders and shake to coat the chicken. Let marinate for 20–30 minutes.

2. Preheat the broiler to 350°F. Prepare a cookie sheet with nonstick spray or coat it with aluminum foil.

3. Sprinkle the sesame seeds on a piece of waxed paper. Drain the tenders. Press the chicken pieces into the seeds on wax paper. Discard the marinade.

4. Broil, turning occasionally, for 10 minutes. Reduce heat to 225°F; bake for another 5 minutes. Serve hot.

YIELDS 6 SERVINGS; SERVING SIZE 3 PIECES

Calories: 140 | Carbohydrates: 3g | Fat: 6g | Sodium: 940mg | Fiber: 0g

Baked French Fries

The nutritional allowance for this recipe allows for the teaspoon of olive oil. You can reduce the amount of oil by half if you spritz the potatoes with oil rather than using the method described in the recipe.

INGREDIENTS

1 small white potato (3 ounces)

1 teaspoon olive oil

Sea salt and freshly ground black pepper to taste (optional)

Can Fries Be Cooked Quicker?

Speed up the time it takes to bake French fries! First, cook the potatoes in the microwave 3–4 minutes in a covered microwave-safe dish. Allow potatoes to rest for at least a minute after removing the dish from the microwave. Dry potatoes with paper towels, if necessary. Arrange the potatoes on a nonstick spray–treated baking sheet. Spray the potatoes with flavored cooking spray or a few spritzes of olive oil and bake at 400°F for 5–8 minutes to crisp them.

1. Preheat oven to 400°F. Wash, peel, and slice the potatoes into French fry wedges. Wrap the slices in a paper towel to remove any excess moisture.

2. Oil the potatoes by placing them into a plastic bag with the olive oil. Close the bag and shake the potatoes until they're evenly coated.

3. Spread potatoes on a baking sheet treated with nonstick spray; bake 5–10 minutes.

4. Remove the pan from the oven and quickly turn the potatoes. Return the pan to the oven and bake another 10–15 minutes, depending on how crisp you prefer your fries. Season the potatoes with salt and pepper.

SERVES 1

Calories: 170 | Carbohydrates: 29g | Fat: 4.5g | Sodium: 15mg | Fiber: 3g

Crunchy Sautéed New Potatoes

Kids love this recipe! It's quick to make and very tasty. The potatoes get quite crisp as the water evaporates and cooks them through. Add fresh parsley just before serving for extra color and kick.

INGREDIENTS

1 tablespoon olive oil

2 tablespoons water

8 medium-sized new potatoes, scrubbed and halved

Salt and pepper to taste

1. Add the oil and water to a nonstick pan over medium heat.

2. Place the potatoes in the pan, cut-sides down. Cover and cook for 10 minutes. Remove the lid and continue to brown until the cut sides are crisp. Turn; sprinkle with salt and pepper.

**YIELDS 4 SERVINGS;
SERVING SIZE 2 HALF-POTATOES**

Calories: 130 | Carbohydrates: 20g | Fat: 3.5g |
Sodium: 0mg | Fiber: 3g

Stuffed Potatoes

Ranch salad dressing is so full of fresh herbs, you don't need to add any more to this excellent recipe. But you could if you wanted to!

INGREDIENTS

3 large russet potatoes

1 tablespoon solid shortening

2 tablespoons olive oil

½ teaspoon salt

¼ teaspoon white pepper

⅓ cup chopped green onions

½ cup ranch salad dressing

1 cup shredded nondairy, vegan
   soy Cheddar cheese

Micro-magic

You can bake potatoes in the oven or the microwave. To cook 3 potatoes in the microwave, cook on high for 4 minutes, then turn over. Microwave for 3 minutes longer, then let stand for 2 minutes; check for doneness. If necessary, microwave 1–2 minutes longer. Let stand for 4 minutes longer before you use or eat them.

1. Preheat oven to 400°F. Scrub and dry potatoes. Rub with solid shortening; prick with a fork. Place directly on oven rack; bake 50–60 minutes, or until potatoes are tender when pierced with fork.

2. Remove from oven and let cool 15 minutes. Then cut potatoes in half lengthwise. Carefully scoop out the flesh, leaving about ¼" shell. Place flesh in large mixing bowl. Add olive oil, salt, and pepper; mash until smooth.

3. Beat in green onions, salad dressing, and cheese until smooth. Fill shells with this mixture, mounding the tops. Place on cookie sheet.

4. Return to oven and bake 20–25 minutes, or until filling starts to brown and crisp. Serve immediately.

SERVES 6

Calories: 370 | Carbohydrates: 35g | Fat: 19g | Sodium: 720mg | Fiber: 4g

Baked Sweet Potato Sticks

These fries are good for you and make a delicious and energizing side dish that substitutes for traditional French fries. Great for kids!

INGREDIENTS

1 large sweet potato, peeled, cut into matchsticks

1 tablespoon olive oil

Salt and pepper to taste

1 teaspoon thyme leaves, dried

1 teaspoon sage leaves, dried

1. Blanch the peeled potato slices in boiling water 4–5 minutes. Dry on paper towels.

2. Sprinkle with olive oil, salt, pepper, and herbs. Bake in an aluminum pan at 350°F until crisp, about 10 minutes.

1 LARGE POTATO SERVES 2

Calories: 130 | Carbohydrates: 17g | Fat: 7g | Sodium: 25mg | Fiber: 3g

Sweet Potatoes Are . . . Sweet!

Full of fiber, potassium, and beta-carotene, sweet potatoes are a healthy and delicious but often neglected vegetable—most people forget about them until Thanksgiving! Their bright orange flesh adds color to any meal. They can be cooked like regular potatoes, and taste best when baked.

Fried Green Tomatoes

*You don't have to be from the South for your child
to love this Southern takeout staple!*

INGREDIENTS

½ cup cornmeal

½ cup all-purpose flour

1 teaspoon baking powder

Salt and pepper to taste

1 egg

¼ cup 2% milk

2 very large green tomatoes

1 cup canola oil (or more if
    needed)

*You can also substitute nonfat milk
    for 2% milk*

1. Mix the dry ingredients together on
   a sheet of waxed paper. Whip the
   egg and milk in a small bowl.

2. Remove stem and core from each
   tomato. Cut tomatoes into ½"
   rounds. Place in the cornmeal mixture; flip each round. Dip tomatoes
   in the egg mixture; return them to
   the meal mixture, coating each side.

3. Heat the oil to 350°F in a deep frying pan. Fry tomatoes until brown
   and crisp. Drain on paper towels.

SERVES 4

Calories: 680 | Carbohydrates: 34g | Fat: 59g |
Sodium: 160mg | Fiber: 3g

Hot-and-Spicy Pork Meatball Sub

To cut back on calories in this recipe, you can make this serve 6 people instead of 4. Make 18 smaller meatballs instead of 16 larger ones and serve them on 6 rolls.

INGREDIENTS

1 pound ground pork

Salt and pepper to taste

¼ teaspoon ground cloves

1 tablespoon Tabasco sauce

2 tablespoons chili sauce

1 egg, well beaten

½ cup fine bread crumbs

½" canola oil (about ¼ cup) in a heavy frying pan

4 hero rolls (whole wheat if possible)

4 teaspoons of your favorite barbecue sauce

½ sweet onion, sliced thinly

1. Mix the pork, salt, pepper, cloves, Tabasco sauce, chili sauce, and egg in a bowl.

2. Form 16 small meatballs; roll them in the bread crumbs. Heat the oil to 350°F; fry meatballs until brown and crisp all over.

3. Drain the meatballs on paper towels. Place on rolls, drizzle with barbecue sauce, and pile with onions.

MAKES 4 BIG SANDWICHES

Calories: 570 | Carbohydrates: 48g | Fat: 29g | Sodium: 670mg | Fiber: 6g

When the Bread Becomes the Serving Dish

Serve this meal with a fork and encourage your child to eat the meatballs out of the sub roll. They may just be full before they eat the bread. Remember, in this case, to hold off on the full bolusing until after the meal.

Grilled Vegetable and Three Cheese Panini

A panini is a grilled sandwich made with a heavy weight on top to squish it down. You can use a heavy frying pan or foil-covered brick on top!

INGREDIENTS

2 baby eggplants, thinly sliced

½ yellow summer squash, cut in ¼" coins

¼ cup Italian dressing, divided

1 sweet red pepper, cored and seeded

2 teaspoons Parmesan cheese, grated

4 slices Tuscan bread (try to get whole-wheat sourdough)

2 slices Muenster cheese, thinly sliced

2 teaspoons Gorgonzola cheese, crumbled

Oil for panini press or frying pan

Branding Your Home Meals

Part of what kids love about takeout food is the name association. If you want, study fast-food menus and rename your recipes to names close to the known name, but with a twist on your own family name. For instance, instead of KFC, if you are the Jones family, you serve JFC.

1. Brush eggplant and squash with ¼ cup Italian dressing; grill until browned in stripes on an indoor or outdoor grill. Grill red pepper, skin side to the flame, until it chars. Place red pepper, while still hot, in a plastic bag. The skin will come right off! Sprinkle veggies with Parmesan cheese and set aside.

2. Spread both sides of 4 pieces of bread with Italian dressing. Load with vegetables and Muenster and Gorgonzola cheeses.

3. Place panini on lightly oiled fry pan or panini press. If using a fry pan, cover it with a second pan or foil-covered brick. Toast the sandwich on medium heat until very brown. Turn if using a fry pan.

4. Cut sandwiches and serve piping hot!

MAKES 2 SANDWICHES

Calories: 430 | Carbohydrates: 50g | Fat: 21g | Sodium: 1020mg | Fiber: 15g

Mini Pizzas with Broccoli and Cheese

Pizza dough is available in most supermarkets, or you can go to your local pizza parlor and buy a pound of freshly made dough, if the pizza maker swears it's sugar free. Or, you can make it yourself and freeze any extra.

INGREDIENTS

½ pound broccoli florets, chopped

1 pound package sugar-free pizza dough

2 teaspoons extra-virgin olive oil

1 teaspoon dried oregano

1 teaspoon cayenne pepper, or to taste

6 thin slices mozzarella cheese

¼ cup finely grated Parmesan cheese

The Secret Veggie Hang Out (Pizza Tops!)

You can make pizza with spinach, asparagus, peppers, or whatever you like. Try using oils infused with basil and/or garlic. The thing is that most kids will eat their veggies when incorporated into a pizza.

1. Preheat oven to 450°F. Blanch the broccoli until softer but still crispy; drain it and set it aside on paper towels.

2. Prepare a cookie sheet with nonstick spray or use a pizza stone for this recipe. Roll the dough out in a 12" × 12" square. Cut into 4 squares.

3. Turn the edges of the dough over by ½" to make a rim. Brush the dough with olive oil. Sprinkle with oregano and cayenne. Spread with broccoli; add the pieces of cheese, cutting the 2 extra pieces to fill in gaps.

4. Sprinkle with Parmesan; bake for 15 minutes, or until the crust is nicely browned.

**YIELDS 4 SIX-INCH PIZZAS;
SERVING SIZE ½ PIZZA**

Calories: 240 | Carbohydrates: 29g | Fat: 9g | Sodium: 560mg | Fiber: 2g

Teriyaki Beef

These skewers also make great appetizers. Prepare them the evening before if you like, then grill or broil just before serving.

INGREDIENTS

Marinade:

¼ cup rice wine vinegar

½ cup teriyaki sauce

¼ cup canola oil

1 tablespoon dry white sherry

1 small clove garlic, minced

1 (1") piece fresh ginger, crushed

Beef:

1½ pounds boneless beef sirloin, cut into ⅛" slices

Wooden skewers, soaked in water

6 cups julienned Boston lettuce

¼ cup of your favorite vinaigrette

½ cup chopped red onion

1. Combine all the marinade ingredients in a shallow casserole dish; mix to combine. Add the beef to the dish and thoroughly coat all the pieces with the marinade. Cover and refrigerate 1–2 hours or overnight.

2. Prepare a charcoal grill or preheat a gas grill to high. Make sure the grill grate is clean and lightly oiled to prevent sticking.

3. Thread the marinated meat onto wooden skewers that have been soaked in water. Cook the skewers 1–2 minutes on each side until the desired temperature is achieved.

4. Serve the hot skewers on a bed of the Boston lettuce topped with the vinaigrette and garnished with the red onions.

SERVES 6

Calories: 430 | Carbohydrates: 8g | Fat: 32g | Sodium: 1070mg | Fiber: <1g

Fried Rice

You can omit the sausage if you'd like and use a tablespoon of vegetable oil instead. If you're not allergic to eggs, add two with the rice and cook until done.

INGREDIENTS

½ pound gluten-free ground pork sausage

1 cup shredded red cabbage

2 sliced carrots

¼ cup chopped green onion

2 cups cold, cooked rice

3 tablespoons soy sauce

3 tablespoons Vegetable Broth (page 183)

⅛ teaspoon pepper

1. In wok or large skillet, stir-fry pork until browned, breaking up meat as it cooks. Drain almost all fat out of wok. Add cabbage and carrots; stir-fry 4 minutes.

2. Add green onions and rice; stir-fry until rice starts to brown, about 5–7 minutes. Add soy sauce or soy sauce substitute, broth, and pepper; stir-fry until rice absorbs liquid and mixture is hot. Serve immediately.

SERVES 4

Calories: 270 | Carbohydrates: 30g | Fat: 11g | Sodium: 1090mg | Fiber: 2g

Chicken Fried Rice

Have everything ready before you start stir-frying, as the process is very quick. All the ingredients have to be prepared ahead of time.

INGREDIENTS

1 tablespoon olive oil

1 onion, chopped

2 cloves garlic, minced

1 tablespoon grated gingerroot

2 cups cold, cooked rice

1 cup frozen baby peas

2 cups chopped Poached Chicken (page 76)

2 tablespoons low-sodium soy sauce

3 tablespoons chicken stock

½ teaspoon dried thyme leaves

⅛ teaspoon white pepper

1. Heat olive oil in large skillet. Add onion and garlic; stir-fry 4–5 minutes, until crisp-tender. Add ginger, rice, and peas; stir-fry 3–4 minutes longer.

2. Add chicken; stir-fry until chicken is hot, about 3–5 minutes longer. Stir in soy sauce, stock, thyme, and pepper. Stir fry until rice absorbs the liquid and food is hot, about 3–4 minutes. Serve immediately.

SERVES 4

Calories: 290 | Carbohydrates: 33g | Fat: 11g | Sodium: 370mg | Fiber: 3g

Chicken and Bean Tacos

Read the package on the taco shells to be sure they are gluten free. Let your family assemble their own tacos so they can pick their own toppings.

INGREDIENTS

1 pound boneless, skinless chicken breasts

½ teaspoon salt

⅛ teaspoon pepper

1 tablespoon potato-starch flour

2 tablespoons olive oil

1 onion, chopped

1 yellow bell pepper, chopped

1 (15-ounce) can Great Northern beans, drained

1 cup gluten-free salsa

8 corn taco shells

2 cups shredded lettuce

1 cup grape tomatoes

½ cup dairy-free vegan sour cream

1 cup shredded dairy-free vegan Cheddar cheese

1. Heat oven to 350°F. Cut chicken into 1" cubes and sprinkle with salt, pepper, and potato-starch flour. Heat olive oil in large skillet and add chicken. Cook and stir until almost cooked, about 4 minutes; remove from skillet.

2. Add onion and bell pepper to skillet; cook and stir 4–5 minutes, or until crisp-tender. Return chicken to skillet along with beans and salsa; bring to a simmer. Simmer until chicken is cooked, about 3–5 minutes longer.

3. Meanwhile, heat taco shells as directed on package. When shells are hot, make tacos with chicken mixture, lettuce, tomatoes, sour cream, and cheese. Serve immediately.

SERVES 8

Calories: 310 | Carbohydrates: 27g | Fat: 11g | Sodium: 690mg | Fiber: 5g

Taco Seasoning Mix

Many Mexican and Tex-Mex recipes call for taco seasoning mix, but commercial varieties often have MSG and other additives. This pure mix is spicy and delicious, and it will thicken sauces.

INGREDIENTS

3 tablespoons chili powder

2 tablespoons minced dried onion

1 tablespoon minced dried garlic

2 tablespoons potato-starch or superfine rice flour

1 teaspoon onion powder

1 teaspoon salt

1 teaspoon paprika

½ teaspoon dried oregano leaves

½ teaspoon dried marjoram leaves

½ teaspoon crushed, dried red-pepper flakes

Combine all ingredients in a small bowl; blend well with wire whisk. Place in small glass jar with screw-top lid and seal. Store in a cool, dry place out of sunlight. Two tablespoons is equivalent to 1 package commercial seasoning mix.

YIELDS 8 TABLESPOONS

Per tablespoon:
Calories: 25 | Carbohydrates: 5g | Fat: 0.5g | Sodium: 320mg | Fiber: 2g

Taco Seasoning Mix

Taco seasoning mix is usually added to tomato sauce when making filling for tacos, tostadas, or enchiladas. One commercial packet is equal to about 2 tablespoons of home-made mix. You can also add it to browned ground beef along with ½ cup of water to make an easy burrito or taco filling.

Tortilla Stacks GF

Crisp tortillas are layered with a rich bean and sausage mixture, then baked with cheese. Yum!

INGREDIENTS

1 pound gluten-free ground pork sausage

1 red bell pepper, chopped

1 (4-ounce) can chopped green chilies, drained

2 (15-ounce) cans kidney beans, drained

2 tablespoons Taco Seasoning Mix (page 248)

1 (8-ounce) can gluten-free tomato sauce

3 tablespoons vegetable oil

9 (6") corn tortillas

1 cup shredded dairy-free vegan Cheddar cheese

½ cup shredded dairy-free vegan Monterey Jack cheese

Corn Tortillas Are Made of Corn, Right?

Not always. You must read the label every single time you buy a package of corn tortillas. Once you're sure they are wheat free, you can choose from many varieties, colors, and flavors. Blue corn tortillas, spicy tortillas made with red pepper, and white corn tortillas are all delicious.

1. In large saucepan, cook pork sausage over medium heat, stirring to break up meat, until browned. Drain well. Add red bell pepper; cook and stir 3 minutes longer. Add chilies, beans, Taco Seasoning Mix, and tomato sauce; bring to a simmer. Simmer, stirring frequently, 10 minutes.

2. In another large saucepan, heat vegetable oil over medium-high heat. Fry the tortillas, one at a time, until crisp, turning once, about 2–3 minutes. Drain on paper towels.

3. On a large cookie sheet with sides, place one tortilla. Top with ⅙ of the pork mixture and ⅙ of each cheese. Repeat layers, using 3 tortillas, ending with tortilla and cheese. Repeat with remaining tortillas, pork mixture, and cheese, making three stacks.

4. Bake 25–35 minutes, or until cheese is melted and bubbly. Let stand 5 minutes. Cut each stack in thirds to serve.

SERVES 8

Calories: 416 | Carbohydrates: 36g | Fat: 20g | Sodium: 1270mg | Fiber: 7g

Egg Drop Soup with Lemon

This is a lovely spicy version of the Chinese staple. Asian fish sauce is made from salted fish, used in place of salt in many Asian recipes. Hoisin sauce is made from crushed soybeans and garlic and has a sweet and spicy flavor.

INGREDIENTS

1 tablespoon peanut oil

1 clove garlic, minced

2 cups chicken broth

Juice of ½ lemon

1 tablespoon hoisin sauce

1 teaspoon soy sauce

1 teaspoon Asian fish sauce

½ teaspoon chili oil, or to taste

1" fresh gingerroot, peeled and minced

2 eggs

1. Heat the peanut oil in a large saucepan. Sauté the garlic over medium heat until softened, about 5 minutes.

2. Add chicken broth, lemon juice, hoisin sauce, soy sauce, fish sauce, chili oil, and gingerroot. Stir and cover. Cook over low heat for 20 minutes.

3. Just before serving, whisk the eggs with a fork. Add to the boiling soup and continue to whisk until the eggs form thin strands.

SERVES 2

Calories: 180 | Carbohydrates: 7g | Fat: 13g | Sodium: 1390mg | Fiber: 0g

CHAPTER 15

Free Foods Worth a Million

Parmesan Crisps GF

Check the crisps frequently while baking—the color should just start to turn golden. Overcooked cheese has a bitter aftertaste.

INGREDIENTS

1 cup shredded (not grated) Parmesan cheese

Freshly ground black pepper to taste

1. Preheat oven to 325°F. Line a cookie sheet with parchment paper.

2. Place rounded teaspoons of the shredded cheese on the parchment, equally spaced with about 2–2½" between each mound. Lightly flatten each mound with your fingertips to a circle about 1½" across. Sprinkle with pepper. Bake, checking after 3 minutes, until the cheese just starts to melt and very lightly begins to brown. Remove immediately and transfer the crisps to a rack to cool. Store in airtight containers.

SERVES 15

Calories: 20 | Carbohydrates: 0g | Fat: 1.5g | Sodium: 90mg | Fiber: 0g

Deviled Eggs

Everyone's favorite—
a great addition to salads or as a whole foods protein supplement.

INGREDIENTS

4 large eggs

2½ tablespoons mayonnaise

1½ teaspoons Dijon mustard

Hot red pepper sauce to taste

Salt and freshly ground white
    pepper to taste

2 tablespoons minced fresh chives

Free, Within Reason

A "free food" in the diabetes world is a food that has few or no carbs. Your child should be able to enjoy these in a smart portion without the hassle or worry of blood checks or boluses. But do watch the portions, because even a 2g carb count can add up if a lot is eaten.

1. Place the eggs in a medium-size saucepan and cover with water. Bring to a boil, reduce to a simmer, and cook for 9 minutes. Plunge the eggs into a bowl filled with ice water. Allow the eggs to cool completely.

2. Carefully peel the shells from the eggs. Cut the eggs in half and remove the yolks from the whites. Place the yolks in a bowl; add the mayonnaise, mustard, hot pepper sauce, salt and pepper, and chives. With the back of a fork, mash all of the ingredients until blended.

3. Fill the egg whites with the yolk mixture using a teaspoon or a pastry bag fitted with a star tip. Serve chilled.

SERVES 2

Calories: 190 | Carbohydrates: 1g | Fat: 15g | Sodium: 270mg | Fiber: 0g

Ham and Cheese Salad

*A hearty entrée salad to be served well chilled by itself,
on top of lettuce greens, or rolled up wrap style.*

INGREDIENTS

1 (¼" thick) slice ham

1 ounce Jarlsberg or Swiss cheese

½ cup sliced mushrooms

3 tablespoons chopped celery

2 tablespoons chopped parsley

1 tablespoon olive oil

1 teaspoon white wine vinegar

1 teaspoon Dijon mustard

1 tablespoon heavy cream

2 tablespoons freshly grated
  Parmesan cheese

Salt and freshly ground black
  pepper to taste

1–2 packets of sugar substitute
  (optional)

1. Slice the ham into strips, about 2" long. Slice the cheese in the same manner. Put the ham and cheese into a large mixing bowl along with the sliced mushrooms, celery, and parsley.

2. Combine the remaining ingredients in a small mixing bowl; whisk together to blend. (You can add 1–2 packets of sugar substitute to make this more of a honey mustard dressing.) Adjust the salt and pepper to taste. Toss ¾ of the dressing with the ham and cheese mixture to coat evenly.

SERVES 2

Calories: 170 | Carbohydrates: 3g | Fat: 15g | Sodium: 370mg | Fiber: <1g

Don't Wash Those Greens (Yet)!

Salad greens should not be washed until just before serving. Loss of vitamins and minerals increases as soon as the leaves are submerged in water. For best shelf life, store fresh greens wrapped in a damp towel in the crisper section of your refrigerator.

Sneaky Crepes

*These tasty "crepes" will surprise you and your child
and quickly become a favorite.*

INGREDIENTS

Cooking spray or margarine for
coating

2 eggs

¼ cup raw chopped onion and
peppers

¼ cup crumbled cooked bacon

1. Grease a microwave-safe dinner
   plate with margarine or spray with
   cooking spray

2. Scramble 2 eggs in a bowl, whipping well, then pour onto the plate.

3. Place plate in microwave and cook
   on high until egg is cooked solid.

4. Sauté peppers and onions if desired.
   Can be served raw as well.

5. Top with bacon, onion, peppers, or
   other toppings and roll up to
   become a "crepe."

SERVES 1

Calories: 200 | Carbohydrates: 4g | Fat: 13g |
Sodium: 320mg | Fiber: <1g

Kid Fizz

Who needs diet soda?
This healthy option will please everyone.

INGREDIENTS

2 teaspoons free exchange jelly or
jam (flavor of your choice)

1 tablespoon water

Ice cubes

16 ounces carbonated water

Another Fizzy Choice

Another alternative to soda is
to mix up your favorite light
drink mix (such as Crystal
Light) and mix it half and half
with carbonated water. Keeping a jug of that in the fridge
means instant access to a good
drink choice at all times.

1. Microwave jam or jelly and 1 tablespoon water on high for 30 seconds to 1 minute, or until jam or jelly melts; stir.

2. Put ice cubes in a 12- to 16-ounce glass. Pour the "syrup" over the ice, and fill the glass with carbonated water.

SERVES 1

Calories: 5 | Carbohydrates: 3g | Fat: 0g |
Sodium: 95mg | Fiber: 0g

Hard-Boiled Egg Salad

*You can add a little cayenne or Hungarian paprika
to add some zip to this traditional recipe.*

INGREDIENTS

3 eggs, hard-boiled, peeled,
    cooled, and chopped

2 tablespoons minced celery

½ scallion, sliced

1 tablespoon chopped fresh dill

2 tablespoons mayonnaise

½ teaspoon Dijon mustard

Salt and freshly ground black
    pepper to taste

Mix all the ingredients together in a
mixing bowl; stir just until combined.
Adjust the salt and pepper to taste.
Serve chilled.

SERVES 2

Calories: 220 | Carbohydrates: 1g | Fat: 19g |
Sodium: 190mg | Fiber: 0g

Hot Mini Stromboli

If you're using wooden toothpicks, soak them in water for 20 minutes prior to use. You could also use metal toothpicks, but stay away from plastic toothpicks, which will melt.

INGREDIENTS

6 very thin slices hard salami

6 very thin slices provolone cheese

6 basil leaves

6 toothpicks

6 teaspoons sugar-free Dijon-style mustard or vinaigrette for dipping

1. Preheat oven to 475°F. Prepare a cookie sheet with nonstick spray. Lay the salami slices on the cookie sheet.

2. Place a piece of cheese and a basil leaf on each piece of salami. Roll them very tightly.

3. Skewer the rolls with toothpicks; bake 6–8 minutes, or until the salami is slightly brown and the cheese melts. Carefully cut into thirds to make 18 pieces.

4. Dip into mustard or salad dressing. Serve hot!

YIELDS 6 SERVINGS; SERVING SIZE 3 PIECES

Calories: 370 | Carbohydrates: 2g | Fat: 29g | Sodium: 1260mg | Fiber: 0g

Cheesy Taco Shells

This clever taco "shell" might just become a family favorite.

INGREDIENTS

Cooking spray for coating

6 ounces shredded cheese
  (Cheddar is best)

Paprika

1. Heat small skillet to medium-high; coat with cooking spray.

2. Pour shredded cheese into pan evenly and allow to cook until edges are brown and cheese has formed into one solid piece. Sprinkle with paprika.

3. Let cool, then slide off onto plate.

4. Fill with favorite taco fillings and fold or roll as you would a soft taco.

YIELDS 1 TACO SHELL

Calories: 690 | Carbohydrates: 2g | Fat: 56g | Sodium: 1060mg | Fiber: 0g

Stilton and Cheddar Cheese Soup

*A very rich soup that goes perfectly with a salad for a full winter meal.
Or it can create a filling and almost carb-free meal with
Parmesan Crisps (page 252) alongside.*

INGREDIENTS

2 tablespoons butter

½ cup finely chopped onions

½ cup finely chopped, peeled carrot

½ cup finely chopped celery

1 teaspoon finely minced garlic

3⅓ cups chicken stock

½ cup crumbled Stilton cheese

½ cup diced Cheddar cheese

⅛ teaspoon baking soda

1 cup heavy cream

1 bay leaf

Salt and freshly ground black pepper to taste

Dash of cayenne pepper

¼ cup chopped fresh parsley for garnish

1. Melt the butter in a large saucepan over medium-high heat. Add the onions, carrot, celery, and garlic; sauté for about 8 minutes, or until soft.

2. Add the stock, cheeses, baking soda, cream, bay leaf, salt and pepper, and cayenne pepper; stir well to combine. Bring to a boil, reduce the heat to low, and simmer for about 10 minutes. Remove the bay leaf. In a food processor or blender, purée the soup until smooth. Add milk to the soup if it is too thick.

3. Serve in warm soup bowls and garnish with fresh parsley.

SERVES 8

Calories: 210 | Carbohydrates: 4g | Fat: 19g | Sodium: 490mg | Fiber: <1g

Popcorn with Hot-Pepper Butter

Try something a little different for a snack. You can substitute other seasoned salts, such as garlic, onion, or lemon-pepper seasoning.

INGREDIENTS

½ cup unsalted butter

½ teaspoon celery salt

1 teaspoon ground cayenne pepper

1 package plain or low-salt microwave popcorn

Mix the butter, celery salt, and cayenne pepper in a cup; heat them in the microwave for just a few seconds. Blend well. Then pop the corn and toss it in a bowl with the butter sauce.

YIELDS ½ CUP OF PEPPER BUTTER (ENOUGH FOR 4 CUPS OF POPCORN); SERVING SIZE 1 CUP PEPPER-BUTTERED POPCORN

Calories: 230 | Carbohydrates: 7g | Fat: 23g | Sodium: 130mg | Fiber: 1g

Spice It Up!

Seasoned salts and spicy peppers will help to vary flavorings for your child. Try different combinations, such as a mixture of celery salt, ground coriander seeds, orange zest, and garlic powder.

Turkey Meatballs

*If you have a party or TV game night planned, you can make these
in advance and either freeze them or fry them at the last moment.
Or prepare and refrigerate, then pop in the oven just to reheat.*

INGREDIENTS

2 cloves garlic, peeled

2 tablespoons chopped onion

2 slices sugar-free bread, such as
    Italian bread, cubed

1 egg

¼ teaspoon cinnamon

1 teaspoon oregano

Salt and pepper to taste

¼ cup grated Romano cheese

1 pound ground turkey

1 cup canola oil for frying

1. Put all but the meat and oil into a
   blender. Whirl until well blended.
   Place the meat in a large bowl; pour
   the mixture from the blender over it.

2. Mix thoroughly; form into 32 meatballs. Heat the oil to 375°F in a frying pan. Fry the meatballs until
   brown. Drain on paper towels.

**YIELDS 32 TINY MEATBALLS (IN STANDARD-
SIZE BREAD PAN); SERVING SIZE 3 MEATBALLS**

Calories: 280 | Carbohydrates: 2g | Fat: 26g |
Sodium: 110mg | Fiber: 0g

Veggies on the Side
Is a Good Bet

Good food must always be
nutritious, served with plenty
of excellent baby veggies such
as grape tomatoes, little carrots, sticks of celery, rings of
sweet peppers, and/or raw
broccoli and cauliflower florets.
Peppers are delicious and have
the most nutrients in red,
orange, and yellow.

Grilled Ranch Chicken

This simple recipe makes chicken that is moist and tender, with a lot of flavor.

INGREDIENTS

½ cup ranch salad dressing

2 tablespoons lemon juice

⅛ teaspoon pepper

4 boneless, skinless chicken breasts

Bolus-Free Dinner? Say it Isn't So!

It is okay, once in a while, to serve a carb-free dinner and allow your child to skip a shot or bolus. Just make sure you count every carb and that it comes in as an actual carb-free meal. Also, the child should have no peaking insulins onboard.

1. In glass baking dish, combine dressing, lemon juice, and pepper; mix well. Add chicken breasts; turn to coat. Cover and marinate in refrigerator 3–4 hours.

2. Prepare and preheat grill. Remove chicken from marinade. Grill 6–8 minutes per side, turning once, until chicken reaches internal temperature of 160°F. Discard any remaining marinade.

SERVES 4

Calories: 280 | Carbohydrates: 2g | Fat: 17g | Sodium: 360mg | Fiber: 0g

Basil Pesto

Most pesto is made with Parmesan cheese and pine nuts,
but a vegan alternative works just as well. And nuts aren't necessary!

INGREDIENTS

1½ cups packed fresh basil leaves

1 cup packed baby spinach leaves

3 cloves garlic, chopped

2 tablespoons lemon juice

½ teaspoon salt

⅛ teaspoon pepper

½ to ⅔ cup extra-virgin olive oil

¼ cup grated soy vegan Parmesan cheese

2 tablespoons water, if necessary

1. In food processor, combine basil, spinach, garlic, lemon juice, salt, and pepper; process until ground.

2. With motor running, add enough olive oil until desired consistency is reached. By hand, stir in cheese and water, if needed. Store tightly covered in refrigerator up to 3 days. Freeze for longer storage.

YIELDS 1½ CUPS PESTO;
SERVING SIZE 2 TABLESPOONS

Calories: 100–120 | Carbohydrates: 1g |
Fat: 10–13g | Sodium: 140mg | Fiber: 0g

Grilled Pesto Chicken

Pesto is a kid's favorite, as most parents discover!

INGREDIENTS

6 boneless, skinless chicken breasts

2 tablespoons lime juice

1 teaspoon dried basil leaves

½ teaspoon salt

⅛ teaspoon pepper

¼ teaspoon garlic powder

1 tablespoon olive oil

½ cup Basil Pesto (page 264)

¼ cup dairy-free vegan sour cream

1. Place chicken breasts in large glass dish. Sprinkle with lime juice, basil, salt, pepper, garlic powder, and olive oil; rub to coat. Let stand at room temperature 30 minutes.

2. Prepare and preheat grill. Meanwhile, in small bowl combine Basil Pesto and sour cream; mix and refrigerate.

3. Grill chicken on oiled rack, turning once, 10–13 minutes, until chicken is thoroughly cooked with an internal temperature of 165°F. Place chicken on serving plate and top each piece with a spoonful of Pesto mixture. Serve with remaining Pesto mixture.

SERVES 6

Calories: 250 | Carbohydrates: 2g | Fat: 14g | Sodium: 370mg | Fiber: 0g

Top Diabetes Centers
in Major Cities

Albuquerque

PRESBYTERIAN HOSPITAL
1100 Central Ave. SE
Albuquerque, NM 87106
(505) 841-1234
www.phs.org

**UNIVERSITY OF NEW MEXICO
CHILDREN'S HOSPITAL**
2211 Lomas Blvd. NE
Albuquerque, NM 87131
(505) 272 5437
http://hospitals.unm.edu

Atlanta

EMORY CHILDREN'S CENTER
2015 Upper Gate Drive NE
Atlanta, GA 30322
www.emoryhealthcare.org

**PEDIATRIC ENDOCRINE
ASSOCIATES**
1100 Lake Hearn Dr. Suite 350
Atlanta, GA 30342
(404) 255-0015
www.pediatricendocrine.com

Baltimore

**JOHNS HOPKINS
CHILDREN'S CENTER**
600 North Wolfe Street
Baltimore, MD 21287
www.hopkinschildrens.org

**SINAI PEDIATRIC
ENDOCRINOLOGY**
2411 West Belvedere Avenue Suite 205
Baltimore, MD 21215
(410) 601-8331
*www.lifebridgehealth.org/chs
.cfm?id=1610*

**UNIVERSITY OF MARYLAND
MEDICAL CENTER**
22 South Greene Street
Baltimore, MD 21201
(888) 567-5468
www.umm.edu

Boston

CHILDREN'S HOSPITAL BOSTON
Division of Endocrinology
300 Longwood Avenue
Boston, MA 02115
(617) 355-6000
www.childrenshospital.org

JOSLIN DIABETES CENTER
1 Joslin Place
Boston, MA 02215
(617) 732-2400
www.joslin.org

**MASSACHUSETTS
GENERAL HOSPITAL**
55 Fruit Street
Boston, MA 02114
(617) 726-2000
www.mgh.harvard.edu

**NEW ENGLAND DIABETES &
ENDOCRINOLOGY CENTER**
40 Second Avenue
Suite 170
Waltham, MA 02451
(781) 890-3610

**UMASS MEMORIAL
MEDICAL CENTER**
55 Lake Avenue North
Worcester, MA 01655
(508) 334-1000
www.umassmemorial.org

Chicago

**CHICAGO CHILDREN'S
DIABETES CENTER**
La Rabida Hospital
E. 65th Street at Lake Michigan
Chicago, IL 60649
(773) 363-6700
www.larabida.org

**CHILDREN'S
MEMORIAL HOSPITAL**
2300 Children's Plaza
Box 54
Chicago, IL 60614
(773) 880-4400
www.childrensmemorial.org

**UNIVERSITY OF CHICAGO
COMER CHILDREN'S HOSPITAL**
5721 S. Maryland Avenue
Chicago, IL 60637
(888) UCH-0200
www.uchicagokidshospital.org

**ADVOCATE LUTHERAN
GENERAL CHILDREN'S
HOSPITAL**
1675 Dempster Street
Park Ridge, IL 60068
(847) 723-5437
www.advocatehealth.com/lgch

Detroit

**CHILDREN'S HOSPITAL
OF MICHIGAN (CHM)**
3901 Beaubien
Detroit, MI 48201
(313) 745-KIDS (745-5437)
(888) DMC-2500
www.chmkids.org

**HELEN DEVOS
CHILDREN'S HOSPITAL**
100 Michigan NE
Grand Rapids, MI 49503
(616) 391-9000
www.devoschildrens.org

Houston

**CHILDREN'S MEMORIAL
HERMANN HOSPITAL**
Pediatric Endocrine Clinic
6410 Fannin, Suite 500
Houston, TX 77030
(832) 325-6516
www.memorialhermann.org

TEXAS CHILDREN'S HOSPITAL
Diabetes Care Center
6701 Fannin Street, 11th Floor CC 1130.03
Houston, TX 77030-2399
(832) 822-3670
www.texaschildrenshospital.org

Los Angeles

**CHILDREN'S
HOSPITAL LOS ANGELES**
4650 Sunset Blvd.
Los Angeles, CA 90027
(323) 361-4606
www.childrenshospitalla.org

NEUFELD MEDICAL GROUP INC.
8733 Beverly Blvd.
Suite 202
Los Angeles, CA 90048
(310) 652-3976

**WHITE MEMORIAL
MEDICAL CENTER**
1720 E. Cesar E Chavez Ave.
Los Angeles, CA 90033
(323) 265-5066
*www.whitememorial.com/services/
diabetes.php*

Minneapolis

**CHILDREN'S HOSPITALS AND
CLINICS OF MINNESOTA**
McNeely Pediatric Diabetes Center and
Endocrinology Clinic
345 N Smith Ave.
St. Paul, MN 55102
(651) 220-6624
www.childrensmn.org

**INTERNATIONAL DIABETES
CENTER–PARK NICOLLET**
3800 Park Nicollet Blvd.
St. Louis Park, MN 55416
(952) 993-3393
www.parknicollet.com/diabetes

MAYO CLINIC
Division of Pediatric Endocrinology
200 First Street SW
Rochester, MN 55905
(507) 284-2511
www.mayoclinic.org

New York City

**MT. SINAI MC
PEDIATRIC ENDOCRINOLOGY**
One Gustave Levy Place
8th Floor
New York, NY 10029
(212) 241-6936
www.mssm.edu

**NYU LANGONE
MEDICAL CENTER**
550 First Avenue
New York, NY 10016
(212) 263-7300
www.med.nyu.edu

**SCHNEIDER
CHILDREN'S HOSPITAL**
410 Lakeville Road
Suite 180
New Hyde Park, NY 11040
(718) 470-3290
www.schneiderchildrenshospital.org

**WEILL MEDICAL COLLEGE
OF CORNELL UNIVERSITY**
525 E. 68th Street
Suite M-602
New York, NY 10021
(212) 746-3462
www.cornellpediatrics.org

Palm Beach

BROWARD MEDICAL CENTER
Chris Evert Children's Hospital
1600 S. Andrews Avenue
Ft. Lauderdale, FL 33316
(954) 355-4400
www.browardhealth.org

**JOE DIMAGGIO
MEDICAL CENTER**
Endocrine/Diabetes Center
1150 N. 35th Ave. Suite 520
Hollywood, FL 33021
(954) 265-6984
www.jdch.net

PEDIATRIC ENDOCRINOLOGY
3400 Burns Rd., Suite 100
Palm Beach Gardens, FL 33410
(561) 624-1985

**PEDIATRIC ENDOCRINOLOGY
CONSULTANTS**
5800 Colonial Dr., #205
Margate, FL 33063
(954) 968-8555

Phoenix

**PHOENIX
CHILDREN'S HOSPITAL**
1919 E. Thomas Rd.
Phoenix, AZ 85016
(602) 546-1000
www.phoenixchildrens.com

**SOUTHWEST PEDIATRIC
ENDOCRINOLOGY, PLC**
9700 N. 91st St., Suite B220
Scottsdale, AZ 85258
(480) 323-4800
www.swpedendo.medem.com

St. Louis

SAINT FRANCIS HOSPITAL
I 55 & Route K
Cape Girardeau, MO 63701
(573) 331-5897

**SAINT JOHN'S MERCY
HEALTH CARE**
615 S. New Ballas Road
St. Louis, MO 63141
(314) 822-PEDS
www.stjohnsmercy.org

**SAINT LOUIS
CHILDREN'S HOSPITAL**
One Children's Place
Suite 11E10
St. Louis, MO 63110
(314) 454-6000
www.stlouischildrens.org

**SOUTHEAST
MISSOURI HOSPITAL**
1701 Lacey St.
Cape Girardeau, MO 63701
(573) 334-4822
www.southeastmissourihospital.com

**UNIVERSITY OF MISSOURI
HOSPITAL, COLUMBIA**
Cosmopolitan International
Diabetes and Endocrinology Center
One Hospital Drive
Columbia, MO 65212
(573) 882-3818 or (800) 500-6979
www.muhealth.org/body.cfm?id=229

Tucson

UNIVERSITY OF ARIZONA
Angel Clinic for Children with Diabetes
1501 N. Campbell Ave.
3rd Floor, #3324
Tucson, AZ 85724
(520) 694-9988
*www.peds.arizona.edu/families/
clinics.asp*

Glossary of Basic Cooking Terms

Active dry yeast

This is a small plant that has been preserved by drying. When rehydrated, the yeast activates and begins producing carbon dioxide and alcohols.

Al dente

A term used in Italian cooking that refers to the texture of cooked pasta. When cooked al dente the pasta is tender, but still firm in the middle. The term literally means "to the tooth."

Bake

To cook in dry heat, usually in an oven, until proteins denature, starches gelatinize, and water evaporates to form a structure.

Beat

To combine two mixtures and to incorporate air by manipulating with a spoon or an electric mixer until fluffy.

Blanch

A means of cooking food by immersing it in boiling water. After blanching, the cooked food is immediately placed in cold water to stop the cooking process. Always drain blanched foods thoroughly before adding to a dish.

Butter

A natural fat obtained by churning heavy cream to consolidate and remove some of the butterfat.

Calorie

A unit of measurement in nutrition, a calorie is the amount of energy needed to raise the temperature of 1 gram of water by 1 degree Celsius. The number of calories in a food is measured by chemically analyzing the food.

Cholesterol

Not a fat, but a sterol, an alcohol and fatty acid, a soft, waxy substance used by your body to make hormones. Your body makes cholesterol and you eat foods containing cholesterol. Only animal fats have cholesterol.

Chop

Cutting food into small pieces. While chopped food doesn't need to be perfectly uniform, the pieces should be roughly the same size.

Confectioner's sugar

This sugar is finely ground and mixed with cornstarch to prevent lumping; it is used mostly in icings and frostings. It is also known as powdered sugar and 10X sugar.

Corn oil

An oil obtained from the germ of the corn kernel. It has a high smoke point and contains a small amount of artificial trans fat.

Cornmeal

Coarsely ground corn used to make polenta and to coat foods to make a crisp crust.

Cornstarch

Very finely ground powder made from the starch in the endosperm of corn; used as a thickener.

Deep-fry

To fry in a large amount of oil or melted shortening, lard, or butter so the food is completely covered. In this dry-heat method of cooking, about 10 percent of the fat is absorbed into the food.

Dice

Cutting food into small cubes, usually ¼" in size or less. Unlike chopping, the food should be cut into even-sized pieces.

Dissolve

To immerse a solid in a liquid and heat or manipulate to form a solution in which none of the solid remains.

Drain

Drawing off the liquid from a food. Either a colander (a perforated bowl made of metal or plastic) or paper towels can be used to drain food.

Dredge
To dip a food into another mixture, usually made of flour, bread crumbs, or cheese, to completely coat.

Edamame
The word for edible soybeans, a green pea encased in a pod.

Emulsify
To combine an oil and a liquid, either through manipulation or the addition of another ingredient, so they remain suspended in each other.

Fatty acids
A long chain of carbon molecules bonded to each other and to hydrogen molecules, attached to an alcohol or glycerol molecule. They are short-chain, medium-chain, and long-chain, always with an even number of carbon molecules.

Flaky
A word describing food texture, usually a pie crust or crust on meat, which breaks apart into flat layers.

Flaxseed
This small, oil-rich seed is used primarily to make linseed oil, but is also a valuable source of nutrients like calcium, iron, and omega-3 fatty acids.

Fry
To cook food in hot oil, a dry-heat environment.

Gluten
A protein in flour made by combining glutenin and gliadin with a liquid and physical manipulation.

Golden
The color of food when it is browned or quickly sautéed..

HDL
High-density lipoproteins, the "good" type of cholesterol that carries fat away from the bloodstream.

Herbs

The aromatic leafy part of an edible plant; herbs include basil, parsley, chives, thyme, tarragon, oregano, and mint.

Hummus

A combination of puréed chickpeas with garlic, lemon juice, and usually tahini; used as an appetizer or sandwich spread.

Hydrogenation

The process of adding hydrogen molecules to carbon chains in fats and fatty acids.

Italian salad dressing

A dressing made of olive oil and vinegar or lemon juice, combined into an emulsion, usually with herbs like basil, oregano, and thyme.

Jelly

A congealed mixture made from fruit juice, sugar, and pectin.

Julienne

Cutting food into very thin strips about 1½ to 2 inches long, with a width and thickness of about ⅛ inch. Both meat and vegetables can be julienned. Also called matchstick cutting.

Kebab

Meats, fruits, and/or vegetables threaded onto skewers, usually barbecued over a wood or coal fire.

Kidney bean

A legume, either white or dark red, used for making chili and soups.

Knead

To manipulate a dough, usually a bread dough, to help develop the gluten in the flour so the bread has the proper texture.

Lard

The fat from pork, used to fry foods and as a substitute for margarine or butter.

LDL
Low-density lipoproteins, the "bad" cholesterol, which carry fat from the liver and intestines to the bloodstream.

Lecithin
A fatty substance that is a natural emulsifier, found in eggs and legumes.

Lipid
Organic molecules insoluble in water, consisting of a chain of hydrophobic carbon and hydrogen molecules and an alcohol or glycerol molecule. They include fats, oil, waxes, steroids, and cholesterol.

Long-chain fatty acids
These fatty acids have twelve to twenty-four carbon molecules bonded to hydrogen molecules and to a glycerol molecule.

Margarine
A fat made by hydrogenating polyunsaturated oils, colored with yellow food coloring to resemble butter.

Marinate
To coat foods in an acidic liquid or dry mixture to help break down protein bonds and tenderize the food.

Mayonnaise
An emulsification of egg yolks, lemon juice or vinegar, and oil, blended into a thick white creamy dressing.

Meat thermometer
A thermometer specially labeled to read the internal temperature of meat.

Medium-chain fatty acids
These fatty acids have six to twelve carbon molecules bonded to each other and to hydrogen molecules. Coconut and palm oils contain these fatty acids, and they are used in infant formulas.

Mince
Cutting food into very small pieces. In general, minced food is cut into smaller pieces than chopped food.

Monounsaturated oil
A fatty acid that has two carbons double bonded to each other, missing two hydrogen molecules. These very stable oils are good for frying but can have low smoke points. Examples include olive, almond, avocado, canola, and peanut oils.

Mortar and pestle
A mortar is a bowl-shaped tool, sometimes made of stone or marble, and a pestle is the round instrument used to grind ingredients in the mortar.

Mouthfeel
A food science term that describes the action of food in the mouth; descriptors range from gummy to dry to slippery to smooth to chewy to tender.

Nuts
The edible fruit of some trees, consisting of a kernel in a hard shell. Most edible nuts are actually seeds and are a good course of monounsaturated fats.

Omega-3 fatty acids
A polyunsaturated fat named for the position of the first double bond. The body cannot make omega-3 fatty acids; they must be consumed.

Omega-6 fatty acids
A polyunsaturated fat named for the position of the first double bond. Too much of this fatty acid in the body can cause heart disease. Like HDL with LDL cholesterol, it works in concert with omega-3 fatty acids.

Organic food
Food that has been grown and processed without pesticides, herbicides, insecticides, fertilizers, artificial coloring, artificial flavoring, or additives.

Pan-fry
To quickly fry in a small amount of oil in a saucepan or skillet.

Polyunsaturated oil
A fatty acid that has more than two carbon molecules double bonded to each other; it is missing at least four hydrogen molecules. Examples include corn, soybean, safflower, and sunflower oils.

Processed food
Any food that has been manipulated by chemicals or otherwise treated, such as frozen foods, canned foods, enriched foods, and dehydrated foods.

Rancid
Fats can become rancid over time and through exposure to oxygen. The fats oxidize, or break down, and free radicals form, which then exacerbate the process. Rancid fats smell and taste unpleasant.

Reduction
Quickly boiling or simmering liquid to evaporate the water and concentrate the flavor.

Risotto
An Italian rice dish made by slowly cooking rice in broth, stirring to help release starch that thickens the mixture.

Roast
To cook food at relatively high heat in an oven. This is a dry-cooking method, usually used for vegetables and meats.

Roux
A mixture of flour and oil or fat, cooked until the starches in the flour can absorb liquid. It is used to thicken sauces from white sauce to gumbo.

Saturated fat
A fatty acid that has no double-bonded carbons but has all the carbons bonded to hydrogen molecules. Butter, coconut oil, and palm oil are all high in saturated fats.

Sauté
To quickly cook food in a small amount of fat over relatively high heat.

Sear

Quickly browning meat over high heat before finishing cooking it by another method. Searing meat browns the surface and seals in the juices.

Season

To change the flavor of food by adding ingredients like salt, pepper, herbs, and spices.

Short-chain fatty acid

A fat that contains two to six carbon molecules. Examples include lauric and octanoic acids.

Shortening

A partially hydrogenated oil that is solid at room temperature, used to make everything from frostings to cakes to pastries and breads.

Shred

Cutting food into thin strips that are usually thicker than a julienne cut. Meat, poultry, cabbage, lettuce, and cheese can all be shredded.

Simmer

Cooking food in liquid at a temperature just below the boiling point.

Smoke point

The temperature at which fats begin to break down under heat. The higher the smoke point, the more stable the fat will be while frying and cooking. Butter's smoke point is 350°F, olive oil 375°F, and refined oils around 440°F.

Spices

Aromatic seasonings from seeds, bark, roots, and stems of edible plants. Spices include cinnamon, cumin, turmeric, ginger, and pepper, among others.

Trans

Latin word meaning "across," referring to the positioning of the hydrogen molecules on the carbon chain of a fatty acid.

Trans fat
A specific form of fatty acid where hydrogen molecules are positioned across from each other, in the "trans" position, as opposed to the "cis" position.

Tropical oils
Oils from plants grown in the tropic regions; the most common are coconut oil and palm oil. These oils are usually fully saturated and are solid at room temperature.

Unsalted butter
Sometimes known as sweet butter, this is butter that contains no salt or sodium chloride. It's used for greasing pans, since salt in butter will make batter or dough stick.

Unsaturated fat
Fatty acids that have two or more carbon molecules double bonded to each other; an unsaturated fat is missing at least two hydrogen molecules.

Vanilla
The highly aromatic seeds contained in a long pod, or fruit, of the vanilla plant, a member of the orchid family.

Vegetable oil
Oils made by pressing or chemically extracting lipids from a vegetable source, whether seeds, nuts, or fruits of a plant.

Vitamins
Molecules that are used to promote and facilitate chemical reactions in the body. Most vitamins must be ingested, as your body cannot make them.